YOUR GOD IS TOO BORING

Jon Leonetti

WELLSPRING

North Palm Beach, Florida

wellspring

YOUR GOD IS TOO BORING

ISBN: 978-1-937509-76-7

Design by Shawna Powell

For more information on this title and other books
and CDs available through The Dynamic Catholic Book Program,
please visit: www.DynamicCatholic.com

The Dynamic Catholic Institute
5081 Olympic Blvd • Erlanger • Kentucky • 41018
Phone: 1–859–980–7900
Email: info@DynamicCatholic.com

10   9   8   7   6

Printed in the United States of America

TABLE OF CONTENTS

SO THERE I WAS. . .

. . .listening to all the canned talking points yet again: Catholicism is outdated. It's behind the times. It's *boring*.

And I had to be polite because they were coming from a friend who didn't know any better.

But inside I was grumbling. Why don't people understand what a mind-blowing truth Christianity really is? Why don't they make the effort to understand that Christianity isn't boring—it's the most dangerous and exciting thing on earth?

And as I was thinking those things, I suddenly realized I had it all backward.

It's not their fault they don't understand. It's our fault for not getting the message out. And we're not getting the message out because many of us don't understand it ourselves. We, the ordinary Catholics who sit yawning in pews all over America, are the ones who need to understand what God and Catholicism are all about. Until we do, we can't do anything to help anyone else understand it.

As soon as I realized that, I knew I had to do something about it.

So I wrote this book.

1. GOD WHO?

Do you know what the longest-running television series in history is? It's not the nightly news. And it's not the weekly sports hour. It's not even *60 Minutes,* or *20/20,* or your mom's favorite soap. No, the world record for longest-running television program belongs to . . . *Doctor Who.* The show premiered way back in 1963, the day after Kennedy was assassinated, and it's still on the air. And you want to know the strangest thing? Fifty years later, we still don't know the main character's name. The title of the series is actually a question. The character simply goes by "the Doctor," to which his new companions invariably respond, "Yes, but Doctor *who?*"

The way we talk about God is like this a lot, too. Atheists, especially, are always lumping belief in any sort of god into one giant category, as though believing in some jackal-headed undertaker (Anubis) or a swan who seduces human women (Zeus) is the same as believing in the God we Christians believe in.

We have people like *New York Times* best-selling author and revered atheist Richard Dawkins convincing people (especially young people) that the story of the God of our Lord Jesus Christ is no different than a lofty fairy tale with magic wands and dangerous potions. He, like many others, has made it pretty clear that an atheist is just somebody who feels about

Yahweh the way any decent Christian feels about Thor or Baal or the golden calf. We're all atheists about most of the gods that humanity has ever believed in, Dawkins says. Some atheists, he explains, just go one god further.

What's our response, you say? Well, that's what this book is about. However, this response, the response of Catholicism, is not just a response to Dawkins. It's a response to all of us—in the pews, behind a desk, or changing a diaper—a response that has captivated the world for more than two thousand years and will continue to do so if we commit ourselves to it.

In order for this to happen, however, we have to first see the problem that many secularists and some well-intentioned Christians seem to share. Simply put, we've misunderstood the story. And when that happens, the entire train gets derailed, boredom sets in, and eventually we become a very, very confused people.

Of course, in fairness to Dawkins and his friends, it took Israel a while to figure the story out, too. Their problem was the same as ours: What do we mean when we say "God"?

Biblical scholars point to a clear development in Jewish understanding throughout the Old Testament. When Abraham is first called by God (Genesis 12:1–3), he is a pagan among pagans, a worshipper of idols among idolaters. But the Lord becomes Abraham's God and the God of his people, and slowly, over time, the Hebrew people begin to realize that God isn't just *their* God—one god among others. God is the only God.

But that took centuries. The prophet Daniel frequently refers to the Lord as "God of gods," and the frequent idolatry that the early Hebrews fell into suggests they certainly didn't *not* believe in Baal and Asherah in the same way that Christians today don't believe in Thor or Jupiter.

It took the Israelites hundreds of years to begin to understand what God is, and Jewish and Christian scholars have been toiling for centuries to understand the existence of God. So, at the very least, when Christians speak of God, the careful listener will ask, "God *who?*" Otherwise, it's easy to confuse the object of their worship with an Israelite version of some animal spirit or superman.

• • • •

God is an extremely difficult topic for conversation. But this shouldn't surprise us, right? I mean, if God is literally bigger, better, and more awesome than anything else—that is, if God is so big an idea that we can't hold it all in our heads—then he can't come easy. In fact, it would make more sense for us not to fully understand God than to fully understand him. Follow me here?

This is precisely what the Catholic Church and the genius minds born from her womb have been tirelessly trying to relay to the world for ages.

You can see now why I roll my eyes when some people today (again, even well-intentioned Christians) present God to the world as some giant Santa Claus waiting to grant us everything on our list or as an aspirin waiting to take the pain away. It's so much deeper than that!

Now, you may be thinking, "OK, so if God is so far beyond my wildest imagination that I can't even come close to understanding who he is in his entirety, what's the point?"

I'm so glad you asked.

The point, and the fundamental difference between Christians and the rest of the world, is that while we certainly couldn't dream of understanding God in his fullness, we can know many things about who he is and how he acts—not because we are really smart, but because he has in fact revealed himself to us. And it's not in some arbitrary, lightning-bolt-while-hearing-strange-voices way. God has revealed himself to the nations as a living person: Jesus the Christ.

You and I *can* know God. It's what the entire story of Christianity is all about. All the distinctions, even the incredibly minute and seemingly silly ones, all the doctrines and disciplines of the faith point to Jesus.

However, before we go there, we have to get the big picture.

There are two basic types of theology in the Christian tradition: *apophatic* and *cataphatic*. Wait, come back! Don't run away yet. The names aren't that important, but the ideas are.

Apophatic theology (from a Greek word that means "denying") begins from the place of God's greatness and why he wants a relationship with us; we might call it "passive" theology, and it's especially popular among Eastern Orthodox theologians. I recently had dinner with an Eastern Orthodox Catholic, who looked at me as we ate and said something profound: "God is a mystery, and I'm OK with that." Many in our culture today might not get how someone can just throw his hands up and "blindly" make such a claim, but I saw it as something very profound and utterly beautiful. You see, this man wasn't saying, "I don't care and I have too many other things to do and I'll just believe there's a God and I'm OK with not knowing any more than that." What he was actually saying was, "God is so far beyond me in all his glory and honor and power and love that I couldn't exhaust even a smidgen of it if I tried. I believe!"

Cataphatic theology (from a Greek word that means "affirming") is the opposite. It's all about what we can say of God: God is good, God is just, God is merciful, God is infinite, and so on. It's "active" theology and what we tend to be more familiar with in the West. But even theologians who focus on those things we can say about God are starting from a place of great humility. They recognize that anything we can say about God pales in comparison to the deeper truth that he is.

Thomas Aquinas, the most important theologian in the West, had an important insight into this as a young boy. He was a really smart kid, but not the kind who had an answer for every question—more like the really quiet, super-smart kid who sat in the back doing something else because weeks ago he'd grown bored with what the rest of the class was working on. His schoolmaster, exasperated one day, finally cried out, "And would Master Thomas have anything to add to the conversation?"

Thomas replied simply, "What is God?"

That shut everybody up. And it wasn't that he was trying to be smart. The point is that the very "what-ness" involved when we start to talk about God is so different from any other we know that even the best of what we say always falls short.

It's a little like when you tell your wife you love her. "How much?" she says. "More than peanut butter loves jelly," you respond. "More than macaroni loves cheese. More than the stars love the sky, or ducks love the water." They're all true, and they do communicate what you're getting at, but they also fall far short of the reality they represent. That's how it is with God.

This is why, at bottom, the God story can never really be boring. As with Shakespeare, it's not so much that it's an acquired taste as that the subject is so big, so deep, so profound that at times what you come up with sounds pitiful.

But it's only pitiful in light of how epic it really can be, and that's how all of our lives are in relation to God himself.

• • • •

When Christians today hear the beginning of Saint John's Gospel, "In the beginning was the Word, and the Word was with God, and the Word was God," they tend to hear that Jesus is in some way attached to the Word—that is, the Scriptures. And this makes sense; after all, Jesus says that he has come not to abolish the law but to fulfill it (Matthew 5:17), that he fulfills the promises to the patriarchs and prophets (John 4:12), and that he is greater than those who came before him (Luke 11:31). That being said, it's not exactly what John was talking about.

The Word—*Logos,* in Greek—means something very different than our English word. It does mean a single word, a single grammatical construct, but it also means word constructs in general. Perhaps the closest word we have in English today is *reason*. So Jesus is the "reason of God," the rationality of God, the method to God's madness. That is very, very important.

That's why faith can never be truly opposed to reason—because Jesus is the source of all reason. It wouldn't make sense for reason to contradict reason, right?

Think about when you and your husband get into an argument. It's generally because one or another of the ideas in question has been misunderstood or misrepresented.

This is precisely how we can understand Catholic theology, not just by itself, but within the culture as well. What science, art, history, philosophy, alternative theologies, social sciences, and pretty much any field that claims to uncover truth misunderstands or misrepresents, the Church corrects—not because the Church presents to the world some alternative idea or invention thought up over lunch one day, but because it presents to the world the one who in fact has been first presented to us: Jesus the Christ.

Christ is the answer!

It's what our Holy Father(s) on down have been trying to get across to the world for ages. That truth is not something I can determine. Rather, truth is found. Truth is Jesus!

I know, the work of unpacking all of this is long and hard and tedious, and few of us have the patience to actually fight the fight. This is why so many who live without God or insist that there is no God at all are so hard on classical Christianity in general, and are often presented to the world as "much smarter" than you and I. And it's not because they've actually out-thunk the faith; it's that many of us have grown too tired or too busy to stay in the conversation.

Those who do stay in the conversation, though, are the ones the Church calls *theologians*. They work in the science of God. They study God and the things of God, the way that he has revealed himself, and the way in which those ideas interact with the other ideas that we have about life, the universe, and everything.

In the past theologians were always considered the most important thinkers, because their job was to think about the most important things and to relate them to everyone else. But now, well, there is a "new evangelization" in town, one that no longer simply leaves everything up to the intellectuals of the Church. (This is where you and I come in.)

What the Church has presented to us is to go out and do precisely what we've been called to do by right of our baptism: make disciples.

That doesn't mean we take the catechism to work each day or read aloud Thomas Aquinas' summa high atop our second-floor deck. That, frankly, would be weird. But we, now more than ever, are charged with the task of helping others see who God really is, and how he has revealed himself to you and to me.

That is what the world is so desperately thirsting for. And it's high time we got to work.

• • • •

Of course, God knew that the mystery of his God-ness would be way beyond us. That's why he didn't give us a philosophy or theology textbook; rather, he gave us the Bible.

It's important to know that the Church presents the Bible to us in a way that's more like a library than an instruction manual. The stories are more akin to those your own family tells at Christmas than to those you see on the Discovery Channel.

The deepest truth that God wanted to reveal about himself was that he was personal, and so he decided to reveal himself in the manner of *persons*—that is, with a series of stories that would make up the history of his relationship with us.

It starts this way from the very beginning. People get caught on the seven days and nights of the first chapter of Genesis and so miss the rest, but this is a little like getting stuck on the fact that Shakespeare wrote in verse. The point isn't the nights and days any more than the point is the rhyme and rhythm. The very fact that the Bible begins with special effects should tell us something about just how exciting this God of ours really is.

What's more, this God that can set stars in the sky and the bounds of the sea; the God who makes sea monsters and the birds of the sky also makes man, for himself. He molds human beings out of the clay of the earth, but he gives them a share in his own divine life by breathing into them. And he gives commands to the human beings that he does not give to the other animals. The others are told, "Be fruitful and multiply." The human beings get that order too (which we still happily fulfill), but are also told to care for the earth. And with this command God establishes a relationship with human beings totally unlike his relationship with all other creatures.

We see this especially in the story of Abraham. Abraham is an everyman, at least by ancient standards. He has flocks and family, and so is wealthy by some standards, but he lacks the thing he most desires: an heir, a son. And so it is that God reveals himself to Abraham, a voice calling out of the night sky and promising the fulfillment of his deepest desire. The voice calls Abraham away from all that is familiar and promises him a homeland and a future beyond his wildest imaginings, and most of all, he promises a son. And the true sign of this God's character? He delivers on his promise: Even in their old age Abraham and his wife, Sarah, are given that son.

There are a number of different lessons to be learned from Abraham's story. God enters our lives at the moment of our greatest need. He answers our deepest desires and prayers. He calls us out of our comfort zones, away from what is familiar and into something bigger, deeper, and wilder than we have ever imagined. He takes us on an adventure, one fraught with danger and in which we, like Abraham, make mistakes along the way. But in the end, if we so choose, God delivers on his promise and we are given the inestimable gift of relationship with him, not because we deserve it, but simply because we have been faithful.

If the story of Abraham "humanizes" God in a certain sense, at least inasmuch as we get to know his character vis-à-vis other human beings, then the story of Moses helps illuminate his deity—highlight his God-ness.

Like Abraham's, Moses' story begins with an adventure (which is part of the reason it's been made into a movie so many times). Moses is called out from among his people. He is raised in royalty though he's the son of slaves. And ultimately he winds up immigrating to another country. And it is there that God speaks to him and gives him that most mysterious of gifts, the Divine Name. This name was considered so holy that the ancient Hebrews wouldn't even speak it aloud, except for the high priest once a year in the holiest room of the holiest building, the temple.

Most of the time when the word *Lord* appears in our English Bible, what it is covering for is this great name, "I am who I am." Even in our not-so-good English construction, which can't really bring out the nuances of the Hebrew, we get a sense of the mystery that surrounds it.

Think about this: When I introduce myself to you I say something like, "Hi, I'm Jon," or more specifically, "I'm a man, husband, father." When God reveals himself to us, he does not present himself as merely another person or thing among other persons or things. He presents himself (wrap your minds around this) as *be*-ing itself!

That's deep.

You see why getting this right is so important. God's name, "I am who I am," reveals as close as we can come to God's own hidden and inner nature.

God and the human person are not the same. If that's true, then it also follows that you're not God (sorry to burst your bubble).

Most of us get that. But the Church goes even further. God's goodness, what we mean by saying, "God is good," is actually of a whole different order, a different category of thought from the "goodness" of you and me. You see, God *is*—not just "was" or "will be," but "is." God, in his very being, transcends even the categories of time and space, which are about as basic as we can know.

Now, that might all just sound like fancy philosophy talk or like a metaphysics prof trying to give a lecture, but try it like this: God is not just a superhuman entity. He's nothing like Zeus or Thor or Loki or Pan. He doesn't have a beard or white hair or sit on a cloud. He doesn't even have a body. What the Catholic Church has presented to the world is that God is the only "necessary being," the "Alpha and the Omega." (Revelation 1:8)

Basically, God doesn't need me. How can he? He's God. He lacks nothing. And if he did need me, he wouldn't be God. How can I fill an already full glass? I, Jon Leonetti, couldn't add anything to the glory and majesty of God if I tried! What can some weak-willed sinner like me add to the one who simply *is*?

So what's the upshot? The best way I can explain it is like this: Every time my wife and I babysit for friends, they try to pay us. We never take the money, though occasionally we might let them treat for dinner later. But whether we get the dinner or not, on our way back to the car, what may seem like a selfless act on my part really isn't always what it seems (don't judge). You see, what inevitably pops into my mind after a night like that is, "Now they owe us."

You've done the same thing, right? Of course, your friends and family think you're super generous, and maybe in some sense you are, but you're also looking out for yourself and your own.

So here's the connection. Though we may think like this, God doesn't. If God *is,* then the very act of creating us is an unmerited gift—a gift we can never repay.

I'm sweating just writing it.

Now, there are some people today, like our atheist friends, who think that simply subscribing to a belief in an entity like God is very, very dangerous. After all, if you start out in some sort of cosmic debt that you already know you can't pay yourself out of, then aren't you just sort of set up for failure?

Well, it turns out it's just the opposite. Instead of being celestial slaves, human beings wind up being the recipients of an inestimable gift—namely, love. Because, while we could have no claim on God, no right to anything at all from him, he chooses to give us not just seventy or eighty years on earth, but life eternal with him, the first, best, and most perfect gift imaginable—heaven! And he doesn't even have to! This is why it doesn't make sense for us to turn away from God. Sin is boring. It's boring because it's less than us and what God has to give us. And anything less than that bores us.

This is the source, the basis, the best definition of love: to will the good of the other for his own sake, and to seek to be united with him to his good.

That's fancy talk for *It's not all about you.*

Love isn't about getting anything in return. It's only about pure gift, exemplified par excellence by your and my very existence!

We'll return to this again and again, but for now simply see it from God's perspective. God willed us into being for our own sake—he didn't need us; we can't add anything to him, make him better in any way, and yet he wills us and wills our good and longs to be with us. And his being with us is the best sort of gift we could ever get. You want proof that God loves you? Take a breath. Listen to your heart. Kiss your baby. None of this needs to be, and if God stopped thinking of you even for a moment it would all just disappear. That's how much he loves us.

But because it's hard for us to see that, he had to show us in an even more radical way—which is why the story of God in the Bible doesn't end in the Old Testament.

The life, death, and resurrection of Jesus the Christ is the final proof of God's existence, his presence in the world, and his love for creation. In the end, it is Jesus who shows us the true depth of God's own character, and the great power he has given us to share in God's own life. "I'm not only going to will you into existence," our Lord says, "but I am going to show you what it means to even exist at all, and I'll do so through my son on a cross." There, we find the truest sense of love, pure gift for the life of the world. There we find our salvation.

What could possibly be boring about that?

2. KNOWING OUR STORY

You've probably had people come to your front door before with a Bible in hand. They always have a verse ready to quote, usually one that tells you why you're going to hell. Or at least they think it does. And they can always tell you exactly what book, chapter, and verse they're quoting. Maybe they go easy on you and just hand you a pamphlet, but most of the time, I'm not so lucky.

While I respect their courage and zeal for their faith, I think many of them have it all wrong.

You see, the Bible isn't just a collection of rules for all occasions. You don't just keep it around so you can look up what to do the next time you have a flat tire. No, Scripture is primarily a story, and the individual pieces—the chapters and verses—don't make any sense unless you know where they are in the story.

That doesn't mean there are no rules in Scripture. "You shall not kill"—that's a rule, and a very good one. "Love your neighbor as yourself"—that's an even better rule, because if you really follow it you don't need to be told "You shall not kill."

But the story is the thing. It's the thing that tells us why there are rules. It's the thing that gives us a context, so we can know what those rules mean. And—most important—it's the thing that tells us who God is.

That's the purpose of Scripture. All those books in the Bible were written over the course of a thousand years or more, by wildly different writers. But God uses them all to reveal himself to us.

And while he's doing that, he holds up a mirror so we can see who we are, too.

• • • •

The story in Scripture is our story, the story of every one of us. It's about you, me, and all humanity.

And it really is the greatest story ever told. There is no story on the face of the earth, no movie, no poem, no book that could ever rival it. None. Zero. Zilch. *Star Wars* doesn't come close. Shakespeare was only pretty good. Homer—meh.

The story begins before the beginning of the universe, and it goes on past the end of the universe. What other story can you say that about?

Our story is important because it tells us who God is. ... The rules don't tell us. They're in there for a reason: We need them because God knows what it takes for us to be happy. But they don't reveal who God is. The story tells us that.

So let's go back to the very beginning of our story, which happens to be the beginning of everything.

The book of Genesis may be the most misunderstood book in the world. There are Christians who use it as a science textbook. If Genesis says the world was made in six days, they say, then that's what you have to believe to be a Christian: six days, meaning 144 hours, not a minute more.

Those Christians tend to shout a lot, so many of the people you meet probably think that all Christians believe that. Naturally, there are atheists who think they can disprove Christianity just by proving that it took more than 144 hours to make the universe the way it is today.

The Catholic position is different, though. Are you ready for the Catholic position? Here it is:

We don't care.

Not that how the universe began isn't interesting and important. But as for the question of six literal days, you can answer yes or no and still be Catholic. Some of the Church Fathers insisted that six days meant six days—and they were great saints. On the other hand, Saint Augustine pointed out that the sun wasn't even created in the beginning, so "day" would have to mean something different—and he was a great saint, too. That's Catholic freedom.

The important thing the first chapter of Genesis teaches us is that God created the world from nothing. First there was nothing, and then there was something. Isn't that what our best scientists tell us about the "big bang"?

The whole idea kind of blows my mind. Scientists can't even think about what there was before the big bang. But Christians have an answer for that unanswerable question: "The Spirit of God was moving over the face of the waters." (Genesis 1:2)

The other really important thing that first chapter teaches us is that God's creation is good. And that's more important—and more controversial—than you might think.

The story of creation ends with the creation of human beings, male and female. Once God did that, creation was complete. And it was very good.

It was up to us to mess it up.

• • • •

Everyone has heard the story of Adam and Eve. So think about this story for a bit. As I said before, you don't have to be locked into the literal truth of it like a fundamentalist. (Although, as I said, there's nothing wrong if you do believe it's completely literal—that's Catholic freedom for you.) The story is more important than literal history, because it's *your* story, and *my* story. It's the story of every human being who ever lived: We know what the right thing to do is, but we do the wrong thing anyway.

That's what happens all the time. God puts us in a beautiful garden and says, "Take care of this garden for me. You can do absolutely anything you want with any of the fruit, *except* there's this one tree, out of all the thousands I've planted, that I don't want you to touch. Go wild with all the rest—eat all the peaches and pears and cherries and tangerines and papayas and carambolas you want, but just leave that one alone. Do you think you can do that for me?"

So what do we do? We get obsessed with that one fruit. We can't stop thinking about it. All the mangoes and guavas in the world are dangling from trees all around us, and the only thing we can think of is that one we can't have.

Does that sound familiar to you?

You know the story from here. That ancient serpent Satan comes up to Eve and tells her exactly what she wants to hear. Go ahead and eat the fruit, he says. It'll make you smart. It'll make you as smart as God. God knows that, and he doesn't want the competition. You're a wuss if you don't. All the cool kids are doing it.

Eve resists for a while, but eventually the serpent overcomes her resistance and she eats the fruit. Then she gives some to Adam, and he—typical male—doesn't resist at all.

And immediately they do become smart, just like the serpent said. Specifically, they become just smart enough to know why God didn't want them to eat that fruit. It wouldn't make them happy; it would make them miserable, and God knew it.

That's a valuable truth about who God is right there. God loves us completely. He doesn't give us rules for selfish reasons. Whenever he wants us to do something, or not to do something, it's because he wants us to be happy, not miserable.

Adam and Eve have really messed up, and God tells them what will happen—pain in childbirth, hard work, and death. God doesn't forget about the serpent, either. "I will put enmity between you and the woman, and between your seed and her seed; he shall bruise your head, and you shall bruise his heel." (Genesis 3:15)

When Christians look back at this verse, they see not just a curse on the serpent, but a promise to Adam and Eve. Some descendant of Eve's will ultimately conquer evil. Can you guess who that might be?

• • • •

Well, Adam and Eve have got themselves tossed out of the garden, but that doesn't mean God doesn't care about them anymore. On the contrary, they go on to have some children. The two brothers, Cain and Abel, each make sacrifices to God, but God doesn't like Cain's, which makes Cain very angry. He looks for someone to blame, even though God tells him squarely that it's no one's fault but his own. "If you do well, will you not be accepted? And if you do not do well, sin is crouching at the door; its desire is for you, but you must master it." (Genesis 4:6–7)

Cain pays no attention to that answer. Somehow, in his twisted mind, it's Abel's fault that God didn't like Cain's sacrifice.

Aren't we all like that?

But fortunately most of us don't go as far as Cain. He murders his own brother, and then tries to lie to God about it. (That never works, by the way. You probably knew that already, but I just wanted to remind you.)

God exiles Cain to wander the world—but even then he doesn't stop caring about him. He promises that he will be safe: "If any one slays Cain, vengeance shall be taken on him sevenfold." (Genesis 4:15)

Meanwhile, Adam and Eve have another son, Seth.

Cain and Seth both have lines of descendants, and seven generations after Cain we find Lamech, who sings the first song recorded in the Bible—a disgusting little ditty about how he'll kill anybody who crosses him. "If Cain is avenged sevenfold, truly Lamech seventy-sevenfold." (Genesis 4:24)

You might want to keep those numbers in mind, because we'll be talking about them again.

Fast-forward a few more generations, and the world is so wicked that there's only one non-wicked family left. So God decides to get rid of all the wickedness in one sweep, with a giant flood. Since Noah and his family are still reasonably faithful, God tells Noah to build an ark and get his family in it, because it's going to rain a bit.

I think we tend to look at this flood story from the wrong point of view. Secretly, I think we see ourselves as the sinners who get washed away by the flood, not as Noah who gets saved in the ark. So we think of the flood as some cruel punishment for sinners. But the Bible writers think of it as a great mercy for the faithful. Even despite our faults, God will still throw us a life raft. Don't sell yourself short—Noah had plenty of faults, too, but God was on his side. For Noah and his family, there was a brand-new earth, washed clean of all the sin and corruption that had made life miserable for anyone who tried to do the right thing.

Sin washed away with water. Does that remind you of anything?

• • • •

Now let's fast-forward a few more generations. A certain Abraham (who called himself Abram in those days), settled for the moment in Haran, gets a message from God. Now, you'd think the first thing he'd have to ask would be the first question we asked: "God who?" There are gods for all occasions, gods to fit any home decor. Abraham grew up in the great city of Ur, the New York of the Middle East, and the main street of Ur was like a shopping mall of temples.

But Abram just gets up and goes where God tells him to go, trusting in God's promise to make a great nation of him—even though he and his wife, Sarah, have never been able to have children. God promises that Sarah will bear him a son, even though she's well past her childbearing years.

We find as we go through his story that Abraham has an unusually friendly relationship with God. Take, for instance, the one time when God warns him that the city of Sodom has grown so sinful that it has to be destroyed. What does Abraham do? He bargains with God as if God were some sort of flea-market vendor. (You can read the story in Genesis 18.)

"What if there are fifty good people in Sodom?" Abraham asks. "Surely you won't destroy the righteous along with the wicked."

And God agrees that he won't destroy Sodom if there are fifty good people there.

"Well, how about forty-five?"

And so on.

Abraham finally talks God down to ten good people. As it happens, Sodom gets destroyed anyway, because the only even moderately good people God can find there are Abraham's nephew Lot and his family, who get a timely warning to get out. But Abraham tried his best.

You can imagine the Israelites telling that story about Abraham's bargain around the campfire and rolling on the ground laughing. It's like Abraham is buying a used camel from God! But they also didn't miss the point, which was that Abraham felt comfortable enough asking God for things to drive a pretty hard bargain.

By now you're well enough acquainted with the God in the Old Testament to know that when he says he's going to do something, he does it. Sarah does bear a son named Isaac, and Abraham just dotes on him. Then one day, years later, God tells Abraham to offer Isaac as a sacrifice. "'Take your son, your only son Isaac, whom you love, and go to the land of Moriah, and offer him there as a burnt offering upon one of the mountains of which I shall tell you.'" (Genesis 22:2)

We often think of this story from Abraham's point of view, but if we think about Isaac for a moment we'll notice something important.

This isn't a helpless little boy we're talking about here. Isaac is a strong young man by this time—remember that he carries the wood for his own sacrifice. And Abraham is a very old man. If Isaac decides not to be sacrificed, there's no way Abraham could hold him down long enough to tie him up.

Isaac has to be willing to be sacrificed. Abraham will have to sacrifice his only son, but Isaac will have to sit still and be sacrificed. And he's willing to do that. He trusts his father so much that he just lets Abraham tie him up. That's how important obedience is to him.

You probably know the story from there, although you may have heard it told in a way that misses the point. Abraham is ready to sacrifice Isaac, and Isaac is ready to be sacrificed. But an angel stops the proceedings, and a ram appears ready for the sacrifice instead.

God himself provides the sacrifice. But Isaac was willing to take whatever God had in store for him.

Obedient to his father even when it means a sacrificial death. Carries the wood for his own sacrifice. Does that remind you of anybody?

If you need another hint, an ancient tradition tells us that the mountain in Moriah where Abraham prepared to sacrifice Isaac, and where God provided a sacrifice in his place, was the hill outside Jerusalem later called Calvary.

When the ancient Israelites told this story around the campfire, they were very much aware that it was at least partly a story of how they were different from everyone else. All around them were people who practiced human sacrifice. The Israelites remembered this story, and they remembered that their God was different from Molech or any of the bloodthirsty deities their neighbors worshipped. Abraham had been ready to sacrifice Isaac, but God stopped him, and then—this was probably the most amazing part—God provided his own sacrifice.

But the Israelites—named for Isaac's son Jacob, who was also called Israel—were never quite convinced that that was good enough. Over and over, they fell into the same temptation: worshipping the gods of their neighbors, bloodthirsty idols that demanded human sacrifice. Over and over, God would send somebody to rally them and bring them back.

That's our story, too. Whenever we run away from God, he is running after us.

• • • •

After a few more generations, we find the Israelites settled in Egypt by special invitation of the Pharaoh. But a new administration decides that the only thing ethnic minorities are good for is slavery. The Israelites live in appalling conditions, and just when you think things can't get any worse, the Pharaoh, fearing their numbers, demands that they deliver up their male children to be killed.

But God hasn't forgotten them. He raises up a great leader, Moses, who takes his people out of slavery in Egypt and leads them toward the Promised Land.

The story of Moses and Israel is also the story of every one of us, and here we're beginning to notice part of what makes the story so much greater than all the other stories in the world. It's a pattern no other story can match—not one. Each part of the whole story is a complete story in itself, but each part fits into the pattern of the whole.

You know the story of Moses, so let's just go over the highlights.

Moses says, "Let my people go!" and Pharaoh doesn't want to let them go. It's hard to give up free labor. So God sends ten plagues, and Pharaoh is more and more impressed. As the plagues get worse, he promises to let the Israelites go, and then as soon as each plague lets up he changes his mind. We get the impression that maybe this particular Pharaoh is a little unstable. He doesn't let the Israelites go until the tenth plague.

The tenth plague is the death of the firstborn sons of all of Egypt. The angel of death passes through the country and takes the firstborn male of each household—but the Israelites have been warned about it in advance.

You're going to be leaving in a hurry, God tells them, so pack your things. Eat unleavened bread, because there's no time to wait for bread to rise. Sacrifice a lamb, and mark your doors with the blood of the lamb. The angel of death will *pass over* those houses.

Saved from death by the blood of the lamb. Does that remind you of anything?

Stunned by the deaths across Egypt, Pharaoh lets the people go. But as soon as they set out, he changes his mind yet again and pursues them with a huge army.

Once again, the people of God are saved from evil by water. God parts the Red Sea for Moses, but the waters overwhelm the pursuing Egyptians.

Moses leads the people onward to Mount Sinai, where God gives them the laws they'll live by. And what does Moses find when he comes down from the mountain? The Israelites have given up on him and on God and are having a big orgy around a golden calf.

God tells Moses he's had it with these people; he'll found a great nation on Moses instead.

But Moses intercedes for the people's sins. He saves Israel from destruction. That's what a real prophet does.

Moses wasn't perfect. He messed up enough that he never got to see the Promised Land himself. But he was still the greatest of all Israel's prophets. "And there has not arisen a prophet since in Israel like Moses, whom the LORD knew face to face, none like him for all the signs and the wonders which the LORD sent him to do in the land of Egypt, to Pharaoh and to all his servants and to all his land, and for all the mighty power and all the great and terrible deeds which Moses wrought in the sight of all Israel." (Deuteronomy 34:10–12)

But Israel knew that someday there would be another prophet like Moses. Moses had said so himself: "The LORD your God will raise up for you a prophet like me from among you, from your brethren—him you shall heed." (Deuteronomy 18:15)

To be like Moses, this prophet would have to know God face-to-face. He would have to lead his people out of bondage. He would have to save them through water. He would have to give them the law from a mountaintop. He would have to intercede with God for their sins.

Does that sound like anybody you know?

• • • •

The Israelites do make it to the Promised Land, but all around them are neighbors who worship different gods—many of them horrible, bloodthirsty idols that demand human sacrifices. But they also know how to throw a party: Many of the idol temples keep sacred prostitutes on hand, because of course that's what the god wants. It has nothing to do with what the priests want.

Israel's constant temptation is to run after other gods. Over and over the people forget about the God who brought them out of Egypt and instead turn to the gods of their neighbors—either the fun-loving ones or the bloodthirsty ones.

And over and over God goes running after them. Whenever the people forget who they are and get themselves conquered by some strong neighbor, God sends a great hero to lead them back to freedom. Then, for a while, they remember that God is their God. But as soon as things settle down, they go running after other gods again.

When we look back at the Israelites in those days, we can see that they clearly don't quite get it yet. They still believe that there are multiple gods, and the one we call God is just one of them. When they're feeling patriotic, they tell everyone that their God is the best god there is. Our God can whoop your god from here to Sunday. But they must think there's something real in those other gods, or they wouldn't be tempted to worship them instead. It will take a long time for Israel to figure out that the one God of Israel is the only God, the God of everyone in the whole world.

After living as a loose confederation for a while, the Israelites decide they want to have a king just like their neighbors' kings. So God sends his prophet Samuel to anoint Saul as king over Israel.

Saul is exactly what everyone wants in a king. He's handsome, strong, a head taller than everyone else, and a born leader.

He also turns out to be a bit crazy, so after a while the Israelites begin to realize that they've made a horrible mistake. After Saul tries to take over the religious part of life as well as the secular, God sends Samuel to anoint David in his place.

King David is a shepherd, born and raised in the little town of Bethlehem. He isn't anything like Saul; he's small and doesn't look like a king at all. When his father, Jesse, hears that Samuel is coming to pick a king from among his sons, he doesn't even bother to call David in from the fields. But God doesn't look at appearances, Samuel tells him. David is the choice.

This "anointing" is the ceremony that makes an Israelite king. The prophet pours a little bit of pure oil on the candidate's head, proclaiming him God's choice, and from that moment he is the "Anointed One"—"Messiah" in Hebrew, or "Christ" in Greek. The one who bore that title was legitimately King of Israel.

David would be known as Israel's greatest king. He was also Israel's greatest poet. He wrote so many of the Psalms we remember that we often call the whole book "the Psalms of David." In his long struggle against Saul, there were many times when he thought he was done for. On one of those occasions he wrote Psalm 22—"My God, my God, why have you forsaken me?" It starts as a cry of despair, but goes on to become one of the greatest expressions of faith in God in all of literature. You should go and read it now. I'll wait.

A shepherd who was also King of Israel, who was born in Bethlehem, whose title was "Messiah," and who wrote the Psalm "My God, my God, why have you forsaken me?" Does that remind you of anyone?

• • • •

The glory of Israel didn't last. David's son Solomon ruled over an extensive empire, but it was already beginning to fall apart before he died. Solomon couldn't hold on to it, and Israel ended up splitting into two kingdoms. The northern one was conquered by the Assyrian Empire, and the people were scattered so thoroughly that they never came back together. The southern one held out longer, but was conquered by the Babylonian Empire, and the people were exiled to Babylon for seventy years.

All these misfortunes came, the prophets told their people, because Israel was always turning away from God. The prophets at least were beginning to get the point: There was only one real God. The idols of other nations were just pieces of rock or wood or metal. But the people of Israel still thought there must be something to them.

The prophets told the people what to expect: Running away from God would only bring misery. But their words weren't all gloom and doom. When things looked darkest, the prophets reminded their people to hope:

> But there will be no gloom for her that was in anguish. In the former time he brought into contempt the land of Zebulun and the land of Naphtali, but in the latter time he will make glorious the way of the sea, the land beyond the Jordan, Galilee of the nations. The people who walked in darkness have seen a great light; those who dwelt in a land of deep darkness, on them has light shined. (Isaiah 9:1–2)

Isaiah's words must have seemed like wild nonsense. The land of Galilee had been the first place to be overrun by conquering empires. It was obliterated. How could a light shine there?
For to us a child is born, to us a son is given; and the government will be upon his shoulder, and his name will be called "Wonderful Counselor, Mighty God, Everlasting Father, Prince of Peace." Of the increase of his government and of peace there will be no end, upon the throne of David, and over

his kingdom, to establish it, and to uphold it with justice and with righteousness from this time forth and forevermore. The zeal of the LORD of hosts will do this. (Isaiah 9:6–7)

This is even harder to understand. A child is born—but he is Mighty God? Everlasting Father? How can we possibly make any sense of that?

Nevertheless, the messages of hope kept coming, even through the long years of exile in Babylon:

> But you, O Bethlehem Ephrathah,
> who are little to be among the clans of Judah,
> from you shall come forth for me
> one who is to be ruler in Israel,
> whose origin is from of old,
> from ancient days.
>
> (Micah 5:2)

Again, how can a ruler come "whose origin is from of old, from ancient days"? These prophets don't seem to make much sense.

• • • •

At last the exile was over. A new empire conquered the Babylonians, and allowed to go back to their homelands everyone who wanted to go. It seemed as though the promises made through the prophets had been fulfilled.

The return from exile isn't the end of the story, though. The age-old problem goes on. Israel is always running after other gods, and God is always running after Israel, sending great leaders to bring his people back to him. The books of Maccabees tell us how the story repeats itself yet again with new pagan villains and new Israelite heroes. And the faithful people of God still look forward to a day when a real king, the one the prophets promised, will arise to bring Israel back to glory. He will be the Anointed One, the Messiah, the Christ.

And here's where the best part of the story begins.

You know how when you're watching a really good movie, sometimes there's a twist that you didn't expect? What makes it a really good movie is that once you know about it, the twist makes perfect sense. In bad movies the twist just comes out of the blue, but in the really good ones, you look back and realize that everything in the movie has been setting it up.

That's what's about to happen in our story. The Christ will show up, just as we always knew he would. But he'll be completely different from what everybody expected.

Yet when we look back on the story, we'll realize that everything from Genesis on has been setting us up for this twist. It all makes sense now.

3. JESUS WHO?

What do you dream of when you dream of happiness?

Do you imagine all the money you could ever hope to spend, and then some?

Do you dream of a huge mansion on the Hudson, with more rooms than you can count and servants to tend to your every whim?

Do you see an expensive car that makes heads turn as you roll down the street?

I think that's the sort of thing most people think of when they think of happiness. For our culture, happiness is always a *what*. It's the thing you would get if you had enough money, or enough power, or enough popularity.

But for Christians, happiness is a *who*. It's a person: Jesus the Christ. And he's anything but boring.

I think one of the problems we're having today is that we haven't been able to tell people who Jesus is, or why he is happiness. I don't think we know the answers to those questions ourselves.

What do we see when we picture Jesus? Most of us operate under the impression that Jesus is some kind old uncle who helps elderly people cross the street, reads smiling children their favorite bedtime stories, and stoops to scratch puppies behind the ear. He lives in a Norman Rockwell painting full of bright colors and smiling faces.

So we try, but we can't really get excited about him. He's definitely a nice guy, of course, but there have been other nice guys in history—Buddha, Gandhi, Martin Luther King Jr., and so on. They were nice, too, and they did some really good things.

The fact is, many are bored with Jesus.

But that's not his fault. If we knew what Jesus was really like, we couldn't possibly be bored with him.

The real Jesus was dangerous. He was revolutionary. He was in your face. He was *alive*.

And he was God.

This is what the Old Testament was preparing us to understand.

• • • •

Right away we see the big difference between Jesus Christ and other nice guys in history. The Buddha was a great teacher and a nice guy, but he wasn't God. He tried to show people the way to happiness, but he never said, "*I* am the way and the truth and the life."

What was the first thing the world heard from Jesus when he started to preach? It wasn't "Be yourself." It wasn't "Smile—it's contagious." It was "Repent, for the kingdom of heaven is at hand!"

What did he mean by that? The only way a kingdom could be "at hand" is if the king himself is here. And the King of Heaven is God.

Who does he think he is, telling us that God is here right now? I mean, God is everywhere, so he's always here, but not so much *here* that you have to say, "The kingdom of heaven is at hand!"

Now, it's possible that Jesus was just an egotistical maniac. That's one explanation. It's not a very good one, though. It doesn't explain why he was willing to give up everything.

So in order to explain this strange phenomenon we call Jesus, we have to know something about him—who he was, where he came from, even how he grew up.

Fortunately, Jesus is one of the best-documented people in ancient history. We have four different biographies of him, written by four different people with four different points of view. Sometimes they tell the same story in the same words, which lets us know they're using the same sources. Other times they tell the same story in different words, which means they probably got them from different sources—or saw the events themselves. And each of the four biographies has stories in it that none of the others have.

We can only wish we had as much information on some of the other great characters in history. If you run into someone who tells you this Jesus story is just a rumor, you can say, "Well, you may be right. But it's at least as likely as that crazy story about Julius Caesar conquering Gaul."

These four biographies (you figured this out already) are the books we call the Gospels, and they're the first four books in the New Testament. You might wonder why Scripture gives us four different stories of Jesus' life from four different perspectives, instead of just one complete story, but I think it's *because* they're from four different points of view. It's important for us to know that these events are *history*, not just stories. And if you're writing an accurate history, you never rely on just one source.

So we'll start at the beginning, and that will tell us something about who Jesus is.

You can open your Bible to the beginning of the New Testament now. And no nodding off, because I know that first page isn't the most exciting, but it's there for a reason.

• • • •

The first thing we see when we open the Gospel according to Matthew is a long list of names. I already wrote about it in my book *Mission of the Family,* but it's important enough to review:

> The book of the genealogy of Jesus Christ, the son of David, the son of Abraham. Abraham was the father of Isaac, and Isaac the father of Jacob, and Jacob the father of Judah and his brothers, and Judah the father of Perez and Zerah by Tamar, and Perez the father of Hezron, and Hezron the father of Ram, and Ram the father of Amminadab, and Amminadab the father of Nahshon . . . Matthew 1:1-17

All right, all right, I know. Your eyes have glazed over already. We won't read the whole thing, honestly.

But why does the New Testament start off with what's basically the most boring chapter in the entire book? I mean, we all know those people who talk about their genealogy all the time. We never invite them to parties.

Well, there's a very good reason for Matthew to begin this way. This genealogy is a summary of the whole story of the nation of Israel. From Abraham, the one who followed God to the land of Canaan, all the way down to Joseph, Jesus' adoptive father, this is the whole story of Israel as a family history.

So the genealogy tells us who Jesus is and where he fits in history. Among other things, Jesus is a direct descendant of David. David was the great king who founded the ruling dynasty of Israel, and the prophets had said that someday a son of David would come, an heir to the royal throne who would make Israel great again.

He may look like a humble carpenter's son now, but Jesus' family comes from a long line of kings.

Both Matthew and Luke tell us where Jesus was born: in Bethlehem, the city of David. Remember the prophecy we heard from Micah:

> But you, O Bethlehem Ephrathah,
> who are little to be among the clans of Judah,
>
> from you shall come forth for me
> one who is to be ruler in Israel,
> whose origin is from of old,
> from ancient days.
>
> (Micah 5:2)

So Jesus is a son of David, and he was born in Bethlehem. Those are two important things we know about him already.

Luke is the one who tells us the details of Jesus' birth—the story we hear every Christmas about no room in the inn and the manger and the shepherds. Luke wasn't there himself, of course, but we have good reason to believe that he heard his stories from Jesus' mother. He practically tells us twice in his Gospel: "But Mary kept all these things, pondering them in her heart," (Luke 2:19) and "his mother kept all these things in her heart." (Luke 2:51) Luke isn't the sort of narrator who imagines what's in his characters' heads. The only way he could know what Mary kept in her heart is if she told him.

So what does Mary tell Luke about her son's birth?

First of all, she didn't get pregnant the normal way. She was engaged to a nice older man named Joseph, but she was just sitting in her room minding her own business when an angel came to visit.

Angels are not cute little babies with big eyes and little wings. Angels in the Bible are terrifying. We know that because the first thing an angel always says when he comes to visit is "Do not be afraid." Obviously he has to say that, because the natural reaction would be to hide under the bed.

So here's what the angel tells her:

> Do not be afraid, Mary, for you have found favor with God. And behold, you will conceive in your womb and bear a son, and you shall call his name Jesus. He will be great, and will be called the Son of the Most High; and the Lord God will give to him the throne of his father David, and he will reign over the house of Jacob for ever; and of his kingdom there will be no end. (Luke 1:30–33)

These few sentences are just full of amazing news. Mary will be the mother of the Son of David—the king everyone has been hoping and praying for all these years. And somehow he's going to live forever, so that he'll always be king. He'll even be called Son of the Most High, "Most High" being one of God's own titles.

Mary, though, has trouble getting over the first amazing thing, which is that she's going to have a child at all. She knows how that usually happens, and she knows a woman can't bear children all by herself. "

And Mary said to the angel, 'How shall this be, since I have no husband?'" (Luke 1:34)

This is a perfectly reasonable question. Is God asking her to marry Joseph right now and get on with it? Is the angel telling her about something that will happen in the far future?

No, it's something much more amazing than that:

"And the angel said to her, 'The Holy Spirit will come upon you, and the power of the Most High will overshadow you; therefore the child to be born will be called holy, the Son of God.'" (Luke 1:35)

"Son of the Most High" is really what the angel meant: Jesus will be the literal Son of God.

Now, this is a bit frightening. Mary is a young girl who's not from a rich family. She's probably intimidated by the town baker, never mind an angel of God. But she thinks it over, and she gives the most important answer in human history.

She says yes.

"And Mary said, 'Behold, I am the handmaid of the Lord; let it be to me according to your word.'" (Luke 1:38)

"I'll do it God's way."

This is the answer Eve didn't give, the answer humanity had been failing to give since the Fall. "I'll do it God's way." It took an obscure teenage girl from the backcountry of Palestine to undo the damage of century after century of doing it *our* way instead of God's way.

We hear the story of Jesus' birth every Christmas, and we know the words so well that we probably don't think about them. Jesus was born in Bethlehem, even though his mother didn't live there, because some bureaucratic mastermind had decided that everybody would have to report to his home city to be "enrolled." (We don't know exactly what this "enrollment" was, but one likely theory is that it was an official oath of loyalty to the Roman government.) Joseph had been born in Bethlehem, so he had to go there, pregnant wife or no pregnant wife. Everybody else was on the road at the same time, so of course the hotels were all booked up, and Joseph and Mary had to settle for the corner of a stable behind one of the inns. (In today's terms, imagine the desk clerk saying, "Well, I don't normally do this, but since your wife is in labor, I'll let you camp out in the parking garage.")

Jesus' birth was strangely incongruous. It's hard to imagine anything more undignified than being born in a stable. Yet angels came to announce the news. But who got that announcement? Not the Roman Emperor, not King Herod the puppet king of Judea, but a bunch of shepherds—poor people who got no respect from polite society. And then, sometime later (it's Matthew who tells this story), three great wise men from the east showed up with presents fit for a king—and they found him in a humble house in Bethlehem.

But, as he had to remind Samuel when he anointed David, God doesn't look at these things the way we do. We expect to find a king in a palace, but more than once God has given us a poor child from Bethlehem for a king.

From Bethlehem, Jesus' family fled to Egypt to escape the wrath of King Herod. (The wise men had very unwisely stopped off at Herod's palace on their way and said, "Hey, do you know where we can find that new king who's going to replace you?" It just wasn't a smart thing to say to a king who was notoriously crazy.) When Herod died, they went back home to Galilee, "the land of Zebulun and the land of Naphtali," which was a land of the ignorant as far as people in the big city of Jerusalem were concerned.

So we know that Jesus was born in Bethlehem, and that fits with the prophecy of Micah. And we know he grew up in the backcountry of Galilee, and that fits with what we heard from Isaiah:

> But there will be no gloom for her that was in anguish. In the former time he brought into contempt the land of Zebulun and the land of Naphtali, but in the latter time he will make glorious the way of the sea, the land beyond the Jordan, Galilee of the nations. The people who walked in darkness have seen a great light; those who dwelt in a land of deep darkness, on them has light shined. (Isaiah 9:1–2)

Galilee was certainly brought into contempt— "Can anything good come from Nazareth?" was a stock joke in Jerusalem.

• • • •

We hear very little of Jesus for the next thirty years. The only thing we know about his childhood is the time he stayed behind in Jerusalem after a family pilgrimage and worried his mother sick. She found him debating with the professors of theology in the temple. He was twelve years old at the time.

After that, the first we hear of him is when he's about thirty years old. In fact, this is where two of our Gospels, Mark and

John, start. And they don't even start the story with Jesus himself. They start with his cousin John, whom we call John the Baptist.

John was a preacher who had a way of bringing in the crowds. They came from miles around down to the Jordan River, where he would tell them to repent their sins and dunk them in the water. He wasn't very tactful—when some well-off theologians showed up, he called them a "brood of vipers," and there's just no way to make that sound polite. They asked him whether he was the Anointed One everyone had been waiting for, and he said he wasn't. "I baptize you with water for repentance, but he who is coming after me is mightier than I, whose sandals I am not worthy to carry; he will baptize you with the Holy Spirit and with fire." (Matthew 3:11; see John 1:25–27)

Then one day Jesus showed up among the crowds, and John took notice. "Behold, the Lamb of God, who takes away the sin of the world!" he shouted (John 1:29).

What could he possibly have meant by that? Lambs don't have much to do with God, and they certainly don't take away sins—unless they're sacrificed.

John had said he wasn't worthy to pick up Jesus' shoes, so imagine how surprised he was when Jesus asked to be baptized. "I need to be baptized by you," John said, "and do you come to me?" But Jesus insisted, so John did as he asked.

> "And when Jesus was baptized, he went up immediately from the water, and behold, the heavens were opened and he saw the Spirit of God descending like a dove, and alighting on him; and lo, a voice from heaven, saying, 'This is my beloved Son, with whom I am well pleased.'" (Matthew 3:16–17)

Remember how John responded when the establishment types asked him if he was the Anointed One: "No, but he's coming." Now here's Jesus coming out of the Jordan, and the Spirit of God is descending on him.

When Samuel anointed David, that act announced him as God's choice; Jesus is anointed by the Spirit of God. We already know that he's a son of David, and the literal Son of God. Now we see that he's the Anointed One—the Messiah or Christ—in a more complete way than David ever was.

• • • •

"Then Jesus was led up by the Spirit into the wilderness to be tempted by the devil," Matthew tells us (Matthew 4:1). Just as he did with Eve, the Devil offers Jesus the chance to be like God. But Jesus says no.

It may not seem like a big deal. Jesus was God, wasn't he? So why should he be tempted by the Devil?

Well, yes, he was God, but while he lived on earth he was also completely human. Have you ever had a really miserable cold? Jesus probably did, too. Did you ever hit your thumb with a hammer and feel like your whole body was made of pain? Jesus was a carpenter; we can be pretty sure it happened to him.

He came here to change the world, but it was going to be hard work. It was going to be the hardest work any human being had ever done. But think how easy it would be if he just, you know, ruled the world! That's one of the things Satan offered him. Just worship me, Satan said, and I'll give you every kingdom in the world. You know I can do it.

Really, Satan can't get over this *incarnation* thing—God becoming man—and it shows.

Jesus has to choose: Will he do it the easy way or God's way? And when he chooses God's way, he's giving Satan the answer Adam and Eve ought to have given right at the beginning.

• • • •

As soon as Jesus comes back from the desert, he starts what we usually call his "public ministry." These days, whenever we hear that word, *ministry*, we think of parish committees, or meetings with PowerPoint presentations. It's such a boring word that we often tune it out.

So if it helps, when we think of Jesus' ministry, we can think of one of the first things John tells us he did:

> In the temple he found those who were selling oxen and sheep and pigeons, and the money-changers at their business. And making a whip of cords, he drove them all, with the sheep and oxen, out of the temple; and he poured out the coins of the money-changers and overturned their tables. And he told those who sold the pigeons, "Take these things away; you shall not make my Father's house a house of trade." (John 2:14–16)

OK, so here's a muscular carpenter with a whip who's scary enough that, with no help, he can send the flea-market vendors flying in all directions, throwing tables over left and right while he shouts, "I won't let you turn my father's house into Kmart!"

Maybe you have trouble understanding it at first, but you've got to admit, it's not boring. And John knew it.

Most of Jesus' ministry didn't involve turning over tables and chasing people with a whip. But I saw a bumper sticker once that read, "When asking yourself what Jesus would do, always remember that flipping over tables is a viable option." It wasn't what he did most of the time, but he was capable of it if he thought it was necessary.

And, really, you only have to do it once or twice to leave a pretty strong impression.

Now, why would Jesus get so angry? (And what does it mean for our parish bake sale?)

It isn't just the buying and selling. These are people who have a nice racket going—one that preys on the poor people who come to the temple to make their sacrifices.

The rules say that a sacrificial animal has to be without blemish. You can bring your own, sure, but then there's a pretty good chance that the priest who inspects it will find a blemish somewhere. But that's OK, because here's a nice shop, right in the temple courtyard, where you can buy your animals guaranteed blemish-free. Yeah, they're a little more expensive, but they're guaranteed. You just sail right through the inspection.

And when you want to pay your temple tax, what do you do? Everyone uses Roman money these days, and that's what you get when you get paid. On the other hand, the temple stubbornly sticks to its own currency, and it won't take anything else. But that's OK, because here's a nice little bank, right as you walk in, where you can get your Roman money exchanged for temple money. Of course, there's a small convenience fee, but what else are you going to do?

John puts this story near the beginning for a good reason. It tells us right away what makes Jesus really angry—in fact, the only thing that makes Jesus really angry—and that tells us a lot about who Jesus is. What makes him angry is when the rich and powerful use God's law to oppress the poor and powerless.

The poor and powerless see how Jesus is on their side, and right away they love him.

The rich and powerful see how much the poor and powerless love Jesus, and right away they think, "We've got to keep an eye on this character."

Now we're beginning to understand the meaning of one of Jesus' hardest sayings: "

> Do not think that I have come to bring peace on earth; I have not come to bring peace, but a sword. For I have come to set a man against his father, and a daughter against her mother, and a daughter-in-law against her mother-in-law; and a man's foes will be those of his own household." (Matthew 10:34–36)

We squirm a bit when we hear that one. Didn't we sing about "peace on earth" at Christmas?

But Jesus isn't telling us what he *wants* to happen. He is telling us what *will* happen. If he turns over the tables of the money-changers, the money-changers' union isn't going to be happy. If you think Jesus was right about the money-changers, you're going to be on his side. If your father made all his money in the money-changing business, he's not going to be happy about that.

You can't just shrug and take Jesus or leave him. That's why he was so dangerous. When people were confronted with the reality of him, they had to make a choice. Either he was who he said he was—the Messiah, the Son of God, the King—or he was an egotistical madman.

You could choose to believe what the world believed, and you could go on with your comfortable life. You might never be really happy, but the world wouldn't hate you.

But if Jesus really was who he said he was, then you had to be on his side. You had to believe that, even though what he was asking you to do was hard, you'd find real happiness if you followed his way.

And that meant the world was against you, too.

4. THE BIG CHOICE

So, madman or Messiah?

Lunatic or Lord?

How do we decide?

There's something to be said for the concept of madness. Jesus certainly didn't make any effort to stick to conventional wisdom. The things he said must have seemed a little bit mad to the people who listened to him. If you accepted what he was saying, it meant that the world needed to be turned upside down. The people on the top should be at the bottom; the people at the bottom should be at the top. He said it himself: "the last will be first, and the first last."

That's crazy talk, isn't it?

But it was the way Jesus lived.

Think what he claimed to be. He was God incarnate, the Messiah, the King of Israel.

So how did he live?

He ventured from place to place on his own two dirty feet.

For three years, he made himself available to anyone who needed him—even the little children.

He talked to lepers and Samaritans.

He washed his disciples' feet.

(Just think of that! In Middle Eastern culture to this day, the feet are considered especially disgusting. More than one West-

ern diplomat has created an international stink by thought-
lessly turning the soles of his shoes to an important Arabian
official.)

And in Jesus' day—especially among working stiffs like
his disciples—the feet probably were pretty disgusting. People
wore open sandals and walked everywhere. There were no
sewer pipes in the cities, and horses and donkeys were all over
the place. Do I need to draw a picture?

> "Jesus, knowing that the Father had given all things
> into his hands, and that he had come from God and
> was going to God, rose from supper, laid aside his
> garments, and girded himself with a towel. Then he
> poured water into a basin, and began to wash the disci-
> ples' feet, and to wipe them with the towel with which
> he was girded." (John 13:3–5)

This is right after the Last Supper, and John tells us specifically
that Jesus knew "that the Father had given all things into his
hand." He is God; he is King. So what does he do? He acts like
a slave.

Peter must think the Master has lost his mind. He's already
worked out that Jesus is the Messiah, the Son of the living God.
Now the Son of God is washing his feet like a common slave!
It just doesn't make sense.

> He came to Simon Peter; and Peter said to him, "Lord,
> do you wash my feet?"
>
> Jesus answered him, "What I am doing you do not
> know now, but afterward you will understand."
>
> Peter said to him, "You shall never wash my feet."

Jesus answered him, "If I do not wash you, you have
no part in me." (John 13:6–8)

Peter has some of the right instincts here. He understands that
Jesus is far above him. He wants to be suitably humble. So he
refuses to let Jesus wash his feet, because that makes Jesus look
like the servant and Peter like the master.

But it's almost comical how easy it is for Peter's mind to
shift gears. His heart is always in the right place, but his mind
lurches from one extreme to the other as he tries to understand. As soon as Jesus tells him, "If I do not wash you, you
have no part in me," Peter immediately decides he wants the
deluxe package: "

> Simon Peter said to him, 'Lord, not my feet only but
> also my hands and my head!'
>
> Jesus said to him, 'He who has bathed does not need
> to wash, except for his feet, but he is clean all over; and
> you are clean, but not every one of you.'" For he knew
> who was to betray him; that was why he said, 'You are
> not all clean.'" (John 13:9–11)

Now, why is Jesus doing this dirty job, especially when he
knows he's about to die a horrible death? He explains it to the
disciples, although they probably only dimly understand it at
the time:

> When he had washed their feet, and taken his gar-
> ments, and resumed his place, he said to them, "Do you
> know what I have done to you? You call me Teacher
> and Lord; and you are right, for so I am. If I then,

your Lord and Teacher, have washed your feet, you also ought to wash one another's feet. For I have given you an example, that you also should do as I have done to you. Truly, truly, I say to you, a servant is not greater than his master; nor is he who is sent greater than he who sent him." (John 13:12–16)

This is how the world looks if you're a Christian. It's upside down. The first are last, and the last first. The Lord comes to serve, not to be served. If the disciples had really digested what Jesus told James and John earlier, they might have understood at once.

You know that those who are supposed to rule over the Gentiles lord it over them, and their great men exercise authority over them. But it shall not be so among you; but whoever would be great among you must be your servant, and whoever would be first among you must be slave of all. For the Son of man also came not to be served but to serve, and to give his life as a ransom for many. (Mark 10:42–45)

This is crazy talk. This is exactly the opposite of the way the world works, and there are people who are prepared to defend the ways of the world to the death. To Jesus' death, at any rate.

● ● ● ●

Yet there were many who kept listening to Jesus, because they could see that his madness was breaking through into sanity. It was the world that was mad.

And whenever people start to get the idea that the world is mad, those in authority begin to worry. It's their job, after all, to keep the world pretty much the way it is—with themselves in power at the top. If people at the bottom start to think there's something wrong with that, it can be very bad for the people at the top.

The last will be first, and the first last? That's the worst nightmare of the ruling class.

And that was what was most dangerous about this Jesus—the way he turned everyone's ideas of right and wrong, wise and foolish, on their heads. I'm just going to lead you through three of his best-known parables, and I think you'll see why Jesus was so dangerous that respectable people decided they would just have to kill him.

First of all, let's look at the context of all three parables, because they come one right after another in Luke's Gospel.

> "Now the tax collectors and sinners were all drawing near to hear him. And the Pharisees and the scribes murmured, saying, 'This man receives sinners and eats with them.'" (Luke 15:1–2)

"This man receives sinners and eats with them." In other words, he hangs around with undesirables. It's always dangerous when someone attracts a large following among society's rejects. The Pharisees and the scribes represent the religious establishment of Judea—often disagreeing, but united in being worried about someone who seemed to call their position of privilege into question.

Jesus heard what they were saying about him.

So he told them this parable:

> "What man of you, having a hundred sheep, if he has lost one of them, does not leave the ninety-nine in the wilderness, and go after the one which is lost, until he finds it?"

> "And when he has found it, he lays it on his shoulders, rejoicing. And when he comes home, he calls together his friends and his neighbors, saying to them, 'Rejoice with me, for I have found my sheep which was lost.'

> "Just so, I tell you, there will be more joy in heaven over one sinner who repents than over ninety-nine righteous persons who need no repentance." (Luke 15:3–7)

First of all, this parable is challenging if for no other reason than because it's about a shepherd. Shepherds had an ambivalent reputation at best.

On the one hand, everyone remembered that David, Israel's greatest king, had been a shepherd boy, and "shepherd" was often used as a metaphor for leaders of Israel. Who can forget "The Lord is my shepherd"? On the other hand, shepherds in contemporary society—that is, in Jesus' own time—didn't command much respect. They were considered notorious thieves and liars, perhaps because their seminomadic life didn't fit with modern ideas of private property. They were so untrustworthy, or at least untrusted, that their testimony wasn't admissible in a court of law.

Then there's what the shepherd does in the story. Leaving the ninety-nine sheep in the wilderness is not the wisest thing for a shepherd to do. The wise thing would be for him to say, "Well, I still have 99 percent of my sheep, and if I can't find one of them I'll just have to make do with the rest." One sheep is pretty much like another, isn't it? And it's better to protect the ninety-nine than to try to save the one.

But shepherds don't necessarily make their decisions that way—and Jesus seems to think that most of the people listening wouldn't either. One thing everyone knew about shepherds was that they were really devoted to their sheep. Shepherds might have been dirty and smelly, and they might have been notorious thieves and liars, but they knew their sheep individually, and their sheep knew them. On another occasion, when some of the religious authorities asked him to say plainly whether he was the Christ, Jesus answered by saying that he had already told them:

> "The works that I do in my Father's name, they bear witness to me; but you do not believe, because you do not belong to my sheep. My sheep hear my voice, and I know them, and they follow me; and I give them eternal life, and they shall never perish, and no one shall snatch them out of my hand." (John 10:26–28)

This was an image everybody understood. "No one shall snatch them out of my hand." The shepherd is fiercely protective of his sheep—not just because they're his only valuable possessions but also because he cares about each one of them.

Now, a well-educated member of the ruling class would say that the shepherd was wrong to think that way. He should think in terms of the benefit of the whole flock, not the individual sheep. He should be prepared to sacrifice the one for the many. If a sheep wanders off in spite of his best efforts, the shepherd ought to let the wolves have it and concentrate on the ninety-nine he still has.

But the ordinary poor shepherd doesn't think like that, any more than you would think like that if one of your children wandered off. "Well, I still have three left," you could say to yourself. But you don't.

The really shocking message of Jesus is that God thinks of us the way we think of our children, not the way a ruler thinks of his subjects. God isn't simply a wise ruler; he is a loving father. The Lord is our shepherd.

Maybe the parable of the lost sheep didn't quite get the point across. So Jesus had another one for them:

> "Or what woman, having ten silver coins, if she loses one coin, does not light a lamp and sweep the house and seek diligently until she finds it? And when she has found it, she calls together her friends and neighbors, saying, 'Rejoice with me, for I have found the coin which I had lost.' Just so, I tell you, there is joy before the angels of God over one sinner who repents." (Luke 15:8–10)

Here Jesus has really gone to the next level. OK, a shepherd was one thing. But a woman? I mean, you realize that this housewife with a broom represents *God*, right?

That smacking sound you hear is a bunch of Pharisees' jaws falling into their laps.

The coin we're talking about is a denarius, which represents about a day's wages for a manual laborer. It's tremendously important if you're poor, trivial if you're rich. The well-off scribes in the audience would probably sneer at the silly woman for turning her house upside down for one little denarius. But the poor, working-class people who heard Jesus knew exactly what he was talking about. Yes, they said, what woman wouldn't do that?

God is like a grubby shepherd. God is like some poor woman with a broom.

Do you begin to see why Jesus is so dangerous to the rich and powerful? He's saying that the poor are more like God than the rich!

• • • •

Well, those were certainly two challenging parables. But Jesus had one more up his sleeve—one that would turn out to be his most popular story ever. The point of it is pretty much the same, but because of the extra detail it's another order of magnitude more challenging. We'll read the whole thing through, because we can never hear this story often enough.

> There was a man who had two sons; and the younger of them said to his father, "Father, give me the share of property that falls to me." And he divided his living between them.

Let's just stop right here for a moment. This younger son is basically telling his father, "I wish you were dead." This isn't just a request for money—it's an incredibly callous insult. Jewish law had very specific rules about how much of the inheritance each son should receive, but it always assumed as a prerequisite that the father would be dead first. Until that time, the sons were expected to remain respectful members of their father's household.

So the younger son tells his father, "I can't wait for you to die." And what does the father do? He gives the son what he asks for, even though his son has insulted him in just about the most disrespectful way possible.

> Not many days later, the younger son gathered all he had and took his journey into a far country, and there he squandered his property in loose living. And when he had spent everything, a great famine arose in that country, and he began to be in want. So he went and joined himself to one of the citizens of that country, who sent him into his fields to feed swine. And he would gladly have fed on the pods that the swine ate; and no one gave him anything.

Right now, the scribes and Pharisees in Jesus' audience probably think they see where this is going. Son disrespects father, son gets what he deserves. Hey, this Jesus character isn't so bad after all! He's got the right idea. We'll have to remember this story to tell the kids.

> But when he came to himself he said, "How many of my father's hired servants have bread enough and to spare, but I perish here with hunger! I will arise and go to my father, and I will say to him, 'Father, I have sinned against heaven and before you; I am no longer worthy to be called your son; treat me as one of your hired servants.'" And he arose and came to his father.

OK, so this story has gone on a little longer than we expected. But the scribes and Pharisees listening to Jesus probably still think this is going to end one of two ways.

It could be that the father will be very just. "You treated me as though I were dead," he will say, "so now you are dead to me." Slam goes the door.

On the other hand, it could be that the father will be extraordinarily merciful and give his son what he begs for. The son spends the rest of his life as the lowest of the hired servants in his father's house, and every father who passes by points and says, "That, son, is what happens to you if you disrespect your father."

> But while he was yet at a distance, his father saw him and had compassion, and ran and embraced him and kissed him.

Wait. What? This is the son who told him, "I wish you were dead!"

> And the son said to him, "Father, I have sinned against heaven and before you; I am no longer worthy to be called your son."

Darn right you're not. You got what was coming to you, you rotten, disrespectful son. Honestly, teenagers these days!

> But the father said to his servants, "Bring quickly the best robe, and put it on him; and put a ring on his hand, and shoes on his feet; and bring the fatted calf and kill it, and let us eat and make merry; for this my son was dead, and is alive again; he was lost, and is found." And they began to make merry.

OK, this is just—I mean, there just aren't words for how wrong this is! Isn't the rotten son going to get what's coming to him at all?

> Now his elder son was in the field; and as he came and drew near to the house, he heard music and dancing. And he called one of the servants and asked what this meant. And he said to him, "Your brother has come, and your father has killed the fatted calf, because he has received him safe and sound."

> But he was angry and refused to go in. His father came out and entreated him, but he answered his father, "Lo, these many years I have served you, and I never disobeyed your command; yet you never gave me a kid, that I might make merry with my friends. But when this son of yours came, who has devoured your living with harlots, you killed for him the fatted calf!"

Absolutely! Hear, hear! The elder son at least has some respect for justice. Maybe this is turning into a story about a father who's lost his marbles, and his good son who talks some sense into him.

> And he said to him, "Son, you are always with me, and all that is mine is yours. It was fitting to make merry and be glad, for this your brother was dead, and is alive; he was lost, and is found." (Luke 15:11–32)

That's it? The story's over?

Well, that settles it. We've got to do something about this Jesus character. There's no telling what other dreadful ideas he'll be putting into people's heads if we let him keep wandering the streets.

If you really want to understand how this story must have struck the scribes and Pharisees, tell it to a bunch of elementary-school kids who've never heard it before. You're pretty much guaranteed to hear, "It's not fair!"

It's not fair—the "prodigal son" (as we've learned to call him) went and wasted everything his father gave him. It's his own fault that he was hungry. The older brother did everything his father asked him to do. He never did anything wrong. But who gets the big party? It's not fair! These are exactly the objections the big brother raises, and we understand them perfectly.

But all those objections come from looking at the story from the outside, using our reason and not our hearts.

If you're a father or a mother, you can see the story from the inside. How many times has your son or daughter insulted you? How many times has she disobeyed you?

Do you think in terms of abstract justice then? Do you say, "This is a disobedient child, who no longer deserves a place in the family"?

No, of course you don't. If your son ran away from home and fell in among drug dealers and prostitutes, you'd worry yourself sick. You'd pray night and day that God would just send him home safe. And if, against all odds, your son did come to his senses, sober up, and come back, you know exactly how you would feel.

The important thing to know, Jesus says, is not that God is just. The important thing is that God loves us like a father— a real father with a heart, not an abstract father dedicated to justice. God loves us more than he loves justice.

And you can see why that's a terribly dangerous idea. The idea of "justice" is what keeps the wheels of power turning. If people don't get what they deserve from God, then maybe there's no good reason why the scribes are at the top of the heap and the shepherds and old ladies with brooms are at the bottom.

Which do we choose? Justice or love? The world as it is or the world as it could be?

• • • •

What Jesus is asking us to do is fundamental. Do we choose him, or do we choose the world?

Well, the world has a lot to offer. The world can give us money, power, and reality shows. What's Jesus' counteroffer? What can he give us that the world can't give us?

"*I* am the way and the truth and the life."

We know somehow that the world isn't satisfactory. None of its treasures are permanent. None of its joys are really joyful.

Jesus tells us, "Choose me. I am the way you've lost. I am the truth you've been looking for. I am the life that you've been missing."

But he knows it won't be easy.

Every year at Christmas we sing about "peace on earth, goodwill toward men." And what does Jesus say about that?

> "Do not think that I have come to bring peace on earth; I have not come to bring peace, but a sword. For I have come to set a man against his father, and a daughter against her mother, and a daughter-in-law against her

mother-in-law; and a man's foes will be those of his own household." (Matthew 10:34–36)

Does this mean all that stuff about peace on earth and goodwill toward men was a lie?

No. God doesn't *will* the "sword." None of that squabbling and fighting is what Jesus wants. But he knows enough about human nature to be able to warn us that it will happen.

Jesus is demanding a radical choice. We need to reject the world and follow him if we ever really want to find happiness.

But the world doesn't want to be rejected. There are too many people who are perfectly comfortable with the way the world is right now. They may not be exactly happy, but they have the things the world thinks are valuable: money, power, fame. They're scared to death to give those things up, and they'll fight hard against any suggestion that they should.

That's why Jesus goes on to tell us,

"He who loves father or mother more than me is not worthy of me; and he who loves son or daughter more than me is not worthy of me; and he who does not take his cross and follow me is not worthy of me. He who finds his life will lose it, and he who loses his life for my sake will find it." (Matthew 10:37–39) Certainly Jesus doesn't want us to break the commandment "Honor your father and mother." The Ten Commandments are still the basis of moral life.

But it could very well happen that if you make the choice for Jesus, if you really live the way he teaches, your family—or friends, for that matter—will reject you. You won't stop loving them, and you won't stop praying for them, but Jesus will be a divider between you.

I pray for everyone who reads this that that never happens. I'm confident that it won't happen for most of you. But for some of you it will.

Are you ready to face that rejection?

There may come a time when the government is on one side and Jesus is on the other. In some ways that happens all the time, but guarantees of religious liberty usually protect your right to disagree with the government. But there may come a time when they don't. Perhaps you sacrifice your popularity for Jesus. Perhaps you choose a life of virtue, which is a constant struggle, rather than the easy way of lust, fame, and greed. Are you ready to make that choice?

If you choose Jesus' way, there will be conflict.

You'll lose friends. (You'll gain friends, too.)

People will tell you you're crazy.

It won't be easy.

Your life will never be the same. You don't know what's going to happen, but you may have to make some very hard choices. You may have to change all your priorities, your Friday night plans, your relationship. You may have to give up your job. You may even have to change your whole way of thinking about the world.

But Jesus guarantees this: It won't be boring, and you won't have to do it alone.

5. A HOSPITAL FOR SINNERS

You may have heard it said, "The Church is not a museum of saints, but a hospital for sinners." It's one of my favorite quotes. If you know me or have ever heard me speak, you know I'm passionate about my Catholic faith. I like to scream it from the mountaintops—which today just means posting it all over Facebook or Twitter. I'm the guy you hate sitting next to on the plane, because I like to talk about it with virtually anyone. Yep, I'm Catholic, and not simply because my parents raised me so—after all, I know plenty of people who are no longer Catholic whose parents still are or at least were (statistically speaking, very few adults continue to practice the faith just for the sake of their parents).I'm not Catholic because it's popular (it's not). I'm not even Catholic because it makes sense to me (it does). I'm Catholic because I know it's my best shot at getting right with God. I believe Jesus. Life is messy—really messy. And Jesus knew it. He knew the struggles of his own day, and he knows the struggles of today. And in that messiness he gave us a Church—a hospital—that offers healing to the broken and mercy to the sinner. It's the kind of healing that brings freedom. Not the kind of freedom in which we can do whatever we want, but the freedom, as John Paul II said, to know and do what we ought. It's also the kind of healing that brings mercy and forgiveness. In my experience of giving talks around the country, I've met many who have a hard enough time forgiving themselves, let alone believing that God can. The Church has offered this from the beginning (John 20:23) and continues today. You see, I need a little help along the way. Jesus knew that, which is why he founded the community he did, a Church that's been there for me and countless others both living and dead.Let's take a look at how it all began, and I think everything will make a little more sense.

• • • •

Mark's Gospel whisks us through Jesus' life at a breakneck pace. He's eager to get right to the point of, well, everything. I appreciate that. It's like a paperback thriller, never letting up till you get to the end. Some evening you should sit down and read it straight through—not as a collection of verses to quote, but as a story. You'll be on the edge of your seat.

Mark starts his Gospel with John the Baptist baptizing Jesus. Then Jesus is rushed off into the desert to be tempted by the devil. After that, he's ready to begin his public ministry.

> Now after John was arrested, Jesus came into Galilee, preaching the gospel of God, and saying, "The time is fulfilled, and the kingdom of God is at hand; repent, and believe in the gospel."
>
> And passing along by the Sea of Galilee, he saw Simon and Andrew the brother of Simon casting a net in the sea; for they were fishermen. And Jesus said to them, "Follow me and I will make you become fishers of men." And immediately they left their nets and followed him.

And going on a little farther, he saw James the son of
Zebedee and John his brother, who were in their boat
mending the nets. And immediately he called them;
and they left their father Zebedee in the boat with the
hired servants, and followed him. (Mark 1:14–20)

As soon as he gets down to work, Jesus calls four fishermen to
follow him.

Why? They're not great preachers—they've never preached
a sermon in their lives. And they don't really have many skills.
To judge by some of the other stories in the Gospel, they
weren't even all that good at fishing (see, for example, Luke
5:5).

Of all the things Jesus would decide he needed right at the
beginning of his career, four fishermen to tag along with him
wouldn't be at the top of anyone's list. Well, almost anyone's,
anyway. Obviously they were at the top of *Jesus'* list.

What was he thinking?

Looking back at it now, we'd probably say he was thinking
of founding a Church.

• • • •

Whatever he was up to, it's obvious that Jesus didn't want to do
it alone. He quickly called others to follow him; John tells us
how Jesus called Philip and his brother Nathanael.

And he found Philip and said to him, "Follow me."
Now Philip was from Bethsaida, the city of Andrew
and Peter.

> Philip found Nathanael, and said to him, "We have found him of whom Moses in the law and also the prophets wrote, Jesus of Nazareth, the son of Joseph."
>
> Nathanael said to him, "Can anything good come out of Nazareth?"
>
> Philip said to him, "Come and see."

"Can anything good come out of Nazareth?" Again with the jokes. People from Galilee were, well, different. They had funny accents and weren't considered smart. It was just like Isaiah told us: "In the former time he brought into contempt the land of Zebulun and the land of Naphtali." (Isaiah 9:1)

But Nathanael would stop laughing pretty quickly when he met Jesus of Nazareth.

> Jesus saw Nathanael coming to him, and said of him, "Behold, an Israelite indeed, in whom is no guile!"
>
> Nathanael said to him, "How do you know me?"
>
> Jesus answered him, "Before Philip called you, when you were under the fig tree, I saw you."
>
> Nathanael answered him, "Rabbi, you are the Son of God! You are the King of Israel!"
>
> Jesus answered him, "Because I said to you, I saw you under the fig tree, do you believe? You shall see greater things than these." And he said to him, "Truly, truly, I say to you, you will see heaven opened, and the angels of God ascending and descending upon the Son of man." (John 1:43–51)

Just meeting Jesus *once* was enough for Nathanael to say, "Rabbi, you are the Son of God! You are the King of Israel!" We get the impression that Jesus smiled or even laughed a little at how quickly Nathanael's cynicism evaporated. You think it's something that I knew you were sitting under a fig tree? You ain't seen nothin' yet!

Philip and Nathanael don't seem to have any special skills, either, unless sitting under a tree telling jokes about Nazarenes is a skill. But Jesus wanted them. He *needed* them.

What was he up to?

• • • •

If calling his disciples to follow him was the first thing Jesus did, it must have been really important. It must have been something that was absolutely necessary to make the whole ministry work.

But why? Jesus was God *incarnate*. Look what he did! He could heal the sick, make the blind see, change water into wine, walk on water, and even raise the dead. What could a bunch of ignorant fishermen and laborers bring to the mission that Jesus couldn't do better by himself?

The key, though, is in what we just said: Jesus is God incarnate. God revealed himself to us in Jesus. This isn't just an abstract idea. It's a concrete fact. If we look at Jesus, we *see God*.

Everyone remembers Jesus' famous "Let not your hearts be troubled" speech. He knows that he will be dying soon, and he knows that his disciples will be facing the saddest and most difficult days of their lives:

"Let not your hearts be troubled; believe in God, believe also in me. In my Father's house are many rooms;

if it were not so, would I have told you that I go to prepare a place for you? And when I go and prepare a place for you, I will come again and will take you to myself, that where I am you may be also. And you know the way where I am going."

He's telling them what will happen just about as explicitly as he can, but the disciples don't get it. They don't seem to be able to understand. They have questions.

Thomas said to him, "Lord, we do not know where you are going; how can we know the way?"

Jesus said to him, "I am the way, and the truth, and the life; no one comes to the Father, but by me. If you had known me, you would have known my Father also; henceforth you know him and have seen him."

How can we know the way? *Jesus* is the way. If you know him, you know the Father.

They still don't get it.

Philip said to him, "Lord, show us the Father, and we shall be satisfied."

Jesus said to him, "Have I been with you so long, and yet you do not know me, Philip? He who has seen me has seen the Father; how can you say, 'Show us the Father'? Do you not believe that I am in the Father and the Father in me? The words that I say to you I do not speak on my own authority; but the Father who dwells in me does his works. Believe me that I am in the Father and the Father in me; or else believe me for the sake of the works themselves. (John 14:1–11)

"Look, you've seen me. That means you've seen the Father. I can't show you the Father any clearer than that."

Jesus shows us *who God is*.

The first thing Jesus did when he rubbed his hands together and got to work was to form a loving community.

If Jesus is showing us who God is, that means *God is a loving community*.

This is the thing that's unique about Christian theology. There is only one God, but that one God is a Trinity of persons—Father, Son, and Holy Spirit:

> "And Jesus came and said to them, 'All authority in heaven and on earth has been given to me. Go therefore and make disciples of all nations, baptizing them in the name of the Father and of the Son and of the Holy Spirit, teaching them to observe all that I have commanded you; and lo, I am with you always, to the close of the age.'" (Matthew 28:18–20)

Without that Trinity in unity, God could not be perfect, because God could not be love. Love needs community.

God not only wants us to know who he is; he also wants us to have everything he has.

You can't just let that one fly by you. It's huge, and it's unbelievable. I'll say it again: God wants us to have everything he has.

Remember, this is the God who created the universe. Everything he has is quite a lot. All the perfection you can think of—that's what he wants for us. He wants us to be immortal, like him. He wants us to be perfectly happy, like him.

Most of all he wants us to be loving—just like him.

Love isn't love without someone to love.

What it doesn't mean is that we're going to be perfect while we're still struggling through life on earth. Jesus knew we're only human, and when he picked his apostles on earth, he picked a bunch of people who were far from perfect.

• • • •

All through the Gospels, we can see that Jesus' disciples just didn't get it. They had no idea what he was going to do with them. Though they lived with Jesus every day and saw what he was like, most of them still seem to have thought that Jesus was going to muscle in and take over the government.

Certainly James and John thought that. One day, the two brothers came to Jesus and asked him for a special favor. (Matthew adds that they brought their mother along with them, and in his version it's the mother who actually does the asking. Probably there was more back-and-forth to the conversation than either Matthew or Mark reports, since they're only interested in the essential point.)

> And James and John, the sons of Zebedee, came forward to him, and said to him, "Teacher, we want you to do for us whatever we ask of you."
>
> And he said to them, "What do you want me to do for you?"
>
> And they said to him, "Grant us to sit, one at your right hand and one at your left, in your glory."

We can see what they're thinking. They've absorbed by now that Jesus is the Messiah. Good for them. But they still think of the Messiah as a conquering king who will restore Israel to a prominent place among the nations.

In other words, they just don't get it.

> But Jesus said to them, "You do not know what you are asking. Are you able to drink the cup that I drink, or to be baptized with the baptism with which I am baptized?"
>
> And they said to him, "We are able."

Sure! What's so hard about drinking a cup, anyway? Maybe it's a big cup. Remember, these are Galilean fishermen who've probably done their share of hard drinking. And as for baptism—well, they work in boats, after all. A little water can't scare them.

> And Jesus said to them, "The cup that I drink you will drink; and with the baptism with which I am baptized, you will be baptized; but to sit at my right hand or at my left is not mine to grant, but it is for those for whom it has been prepared."

This answer satisfied nobody. James and John didn't know what to make of it, and their mother probably pestered them with questions like "Are you sure this career has any path for advancement? Your cousin's a doctor, you know."

Worse than that, the rest of the disciples heard about what James and John had done, and they weren't too happy. Cold stares followed the brothers for some time. Who did they think they were, anyway?

In other words, the other ten didn't get it either.

> And when the ten heard it, they began to be indignant at James and John. And Jesus called them to him and said to them, "You know that those who are supposed to rule over the Gentiles lord it over them, and their great men exercise authority over them. But it shall not be so among you; but whoever would be great among you must be your servant, and whoever would be first among you must be slave of all. For the Son of man also came not to be served but to serve, and to give his life as a ransom for many." (Mark 10:35–45)

Oh, here's all that world-turned-upside-down stuff again. The first will be last and so on. We can be pretty sure it went right over their heads. OK, so we can say that Jesus didn't pick the brightest crayons in the box to be his disciples. They consistently misunderstood him, they said and did the wrong things at the wrong times, and they bickered and jostled for the top spots in the kingdom. And to top it all off, they were sinners.

But at least they were guys he could rely on, right?

Well, actually, the only one who followed Jesus to the foot of the cross was John. The others almost tripped over each other running away when he was in trouble.

What kind of Church is he starting?

• • • •

The twelve disciples weren't the only members of the community. Jesus would never have been arrested if he had just been a crank with a dozen other cranks following him. He was arrested because he was changing the lives of thousands of people, and hundreds of them counted themselves as his followers.

Many of his followers were women, which was scandalous in itself. Proper Jewish men didn't talk to women. Certainly women didn't sit in on the lectures by popular rabbis—it just wasn't done.

Other followers were Samaritans, which was even worse. Jews refused to have anything to do with Samaritans, the descendants of the lowest-class Israelites and the outside colonists who were brought in to repopulate Samaria when the Assyrian Empire ejected all the important people in Israel. For that matter, Samaritans wouldn't have anything to do with Jews, either. Yet this Jesus had followers among the Samaritans.

Worst of all, some of Jesus' followers were *Samaritan women*.

This was a really disreputable community Jesus was building up.

It did have some well-to-do members. Lazarus and his sisters Mary and Martha, for example, seem to have been quite comfortable, with a nice house where Jesus and his disciples could stay when they came to Bethany. And of course there was Joseph of Arimathea, a respectable gentleman who had a fine tomb ready for himself that he gave to Jesus instead.

But the community was also full of outcasts—Samaritans, tax collectors (thieves), women you'd never let your son go out with. Jesus treated them all as if they were just as good as the decent, upstanding citizens.

What could he hope to gain that way? Why didn't he pick competent administrators from the most educated classes?

How did he expect to get anywhere with this movement of his, whatever it was, if he filled it with people like *that?*

• • • •

Peter was probably the most consistently wrongheaded of Christ's disciples. At first, he did just about everything wrong (we have a lot in common). He constantly misunderstood Jesus. He didn't get it. He babbled incoherently at the Transfiguration, "not knowing what he said," as Luke politely puts it (Luke 9:33). He resorted to violence and had to be put in his place. Even when he finally seemed to be getting it, he was still wide of the mark:

> "Then Peter came up and said to him, 'Lord, how often shall my brother sin against me, and I forgive him? As many as seven times?'
>
> Jesus said to him, 'I do not say to you seven times, but seventy times seven.'" (Matthew 18:21–22)

Do you remember the song of Lamech, by the way? "If Cain is avenged sevenfold, truly Lamech seventy-sevenfold." (Genesis 4:24)

That's the world's idea of how to deal with an insult: Your honor is at stake! Peter has begun to figure out, finally, that the way of the world isn't Jesus' way. But he isn't quite prepared to hear Jesus turn the world completely upside down. Not revenge seventy-seven times, but forgiveness seventy times seven! (In the Greek translation familiar to the New Testament writers, by the way, Lamech says "seventy times seven," which makes Jesus' remark even more obviously a reference to the song of Lamech.)

So Peter was a loose cannon and a bit dense. I heard some-body once call him the patron saint of goof-ups. (You see why he is my favorite!)

And what was his worst goof of all? He denied Jesus three times. What's the difference between Peter and Judas, any-way? Judas betrayed Jesus, but after Jesus was arrested Peter said, "Jesus who? I have no idea who you're talking about." That's not much better. If that isn't a betrayal, what is?

• • • •

So what *is* the difference between Peter and Judas?

Judas betrayed Jesus by leading the soldiers to him. Peter betrayed Jesus by telling everyone who asked that he'd never met that crazy street preacher.

But the difference is in how each dealt with his betrayal. Ju-das despaired. He didn't think anyone could ever forgive him for what he'd done. He stayed away from all his friends, and went out alone into a field to kill himself.

Peter stayed with his friends—the Church, the community Jesus had founded. He knew how badly he'd messed up, but he trusted that somehow he could be forgiven.

Alone, Judas killed himself. In community, Peter overcame his weaknesses and flourished.

And he would continue to flourish in that community, in spite of setbacks. He was still the same old Peter. He had a nasty public argument with Paul about whether Christians had to keep the Jewish law—and had to admit later that Paul was right and he was wrong. The ancient tradition tells us that he ran away from the great persecution in Rome, leaving his friends to fend for themselves—but turned back when he met

Jesus on the road out of Rome, heading back to the city "to be crucified again," as he told his old friend.

But with all his flaws, Peter was the one Jesus chose to be leader of his Church. And he was a great leader—not because he didn't make mistakes, but because he held everyone together. During the thirty-five years or so when Peter was the leader of the Church, it grew from maybe a few hundred people in Palestine to tens of thousands all over the Roman world.

And what was that early Church like? We know a lot about that, because Saint Luke—the same one who wrote the Gospel that bears his name—wrote a history of the earliest days of the Church. It's in our Bible now under the title Acts of the Apostles. Right near the beginning of the book, this is how he describes the Christians' life:

> And they devoted themselves to the apostles' teaching and fellowship, to the breaking of bread and the prayers. And fear came upon every soul; and many wonders and signs were done through the apostles. And all who believed were together and had all things in common; and they sold their possessions and goods and distributed them to all, as any had need. And day by day, attending the temple together and breaking bread in their homes, they partook of food with glad and generous hearts, praising God and having favor with all the people. And the Lord added to their number day by day those who were being saved. (Acts 2:41–47)

This is a picture of the Church just weeks after Christ had ascended into heaven. Doesn't it look like the Catholic Church today?

Look how the Christians spent their time.

They went to the temple to worship. We can't do that, because the temple was destroyed about forty years later, and even before that the temple authorities had thrown out the Christians. But we do have our own places of worship, where the only true sacrifice—the Eucharist, the sacrament Jesus instituted at the Last Supper—happens every day.

They broke bread together in their homes, meaning they were celebrating the Eucharist. Later, when the temple was closed to them, the Christians would have all their prayers in their own homes, or, as their numbers grew, in buildings they set aside for their assemblies—in other words, their local churches.

They "devoted themselves to the Apostles' teaching and fellowship, to the breaking of bread and the prayers." (Acts 2:42) This is still a good description of our liturgy today. We hear the Scriptures, including the letters of the apostles themselves. We hear teaching from a priest, who represents the bishop of the diocese—and the bishop is one of the successors of the apostles. We take up an offering for the needs of the Church and the poor. Then we have the breaking of bread—the Eucharist. And we offer prayers for ourselves and the whole world.

It's important to notice these things because there are people today—people who apparently don't quite know their history—who will tell you that the Catholic Church is a medieval invention, and it's nothing like "primitive Christianity."

How do you answer those people? You point to the Gospels, and you point to Acts.

The first thing Jesus did when he started his ministry was to form a community. The first thing that community did when Jesus left them in charge of spreading the Gospel was to act like a Church—and not just any Church, but the one, holy, catholic, and apostolic Church. We can recognize it right there in the second chapter of the Acts of the Apostles.

• • • •

Well, you can't argue with success. No matter how unlikely the community Jesus founded, it has a billion members now. That's the largest single religious group in the world.

In just that first generation, the growth was tremendous. From 120 people, the Church had grown to tens of thousands by the time Peter and Paul died.

So if Peter was such a goof-up, what made him such a phenomenally effective leader? I mean, if you were on some corporate board and you heard that someone had made an organization grow that much in thirty years, you'd be offering him the big bucks to be your CEO.

But the fact is that Peter himself had very little to do with it. He did the work, but he didn't provide the power. Jesus made a promise just before he ascended: "But you shall receive power when the Holy Spirit has come upon you." (Acts 1:8) He didn't say, "You'll be perfect," or "Everything that's wrong with you will disappear." But he did promise his apostles power.

And power was what they got—the power to accomplish whatever their Lord asked of them.

Living as a Catholic doesn't mean keeping our eyes turned upward all the time. It means strapping on our suspenders and getting to work with our eyes on each other.

Love your neighbor as yourself. If you can do that, you really do have the best thing God can give you—you're actually becoming like God.

And if that isn't exciting, I don't know what is.

6. LET THE FIRE FALL

The Acts of the Apostles begins with Jesus ascending into heaven. That's a pretty big deal.

And then what happens?

Well, the apostles pray and do some administrative stuff. For instance, they have to pick someone to replace Judas, so they get that out of the way, and then they get back to more praying, "together with the women and Mary the mother of Jesus, and with his brothers." (Acts 1:14) Luke tells us that, all told, there were about 120 Christians at that point. That's nine Christians for every apostle, which sort of makes a bishop's work easy. Mostly they all just sit around in that big upstairs room where Jesus celebrated the Last Supper with his disciples. It doesn't sound like a very exciting life.

But that's just chapter 1. The fireworks start in chapter 2.

• • • •

"When the day of Pentecost had come, they were all together in one place. And suddenly a sound came from heaven like the rush of a mighty wind, and it filled all the house where they were sitting. And there appeared to them tongues as of fire, distributed and resting on each one of them." (Acts 2:1–3)

OK, now we're getting into the special effects.

"And they were all filled with the Holy Spirit and began to speak in other tongues, as the Spirit gave them utterance.

Now there were dwelling in Jerusalem Jews, devout men from every nation under heaven." (Acts 2:4–5)

We should stop for a bit of context here. By this time the Jews were spread out over practically the whole inhabited world—as they still are, of course. There were Jews in every part of the Roman Empire, and there were Jews in all the neighboring countries, and there were Jews as far away as India and Ethiopia. They kept their identity as Jews, but they all grew up speaking the languages of the places they lived in.

This is definitely an audience ripe for hearing the Good News. It's exactly the right opportunity for following Jesus' last instructions: "Go therefore and make disciples of all nations, baptizing them in the name of the Father and of the Son and of the Holy Spirit, teaching them to observe all that I have commanded you." (Matthew 28:19–20) But until now the apostles have just been sitting around.

Then comes the fire.

Fire is a powerful thing. It can be fearfully powerful, but it's also amazingly useful.

In the Bible, fire is usually purifying. God is like "a refiner's fire," (Malachi 3:2) burning up all the impurities and leaving the pure gold behind. When gold (or pretty much any other metal) comes out of the ground, it comes as ore, fused with other minerals. In other words, it's all mixed up with useless junk. It's imprisoned in worthlessness.

What the refiner has to do is set the gold free. And fire is what does it. It takes away the things that keep gold from being golden. It sets the gold free to sparkle and shine.

And that's what the fire of the Spirit does. It burns up fear, despair, laziness, pride—all the things that hold us back and keep us from getting God's work done. It leaves us purified and free. Then we can be the people God always meant us to be—we can let Christ live in us, instead of blocking the door with all our irrelevant earthly concerns. "I have been crucified with Christ; it is no longer I who live, but Christ who lives in me; and the life I now live in the flesh I live by faith in the Son of God, who loved me and gave himself for me." (Galatians 2:20)

Now comes the paragraph that's every lector's worst nightmare at Mass:

> And at this sound the multitude came together, and they were bewildered, because each one heard them speaking in his own language. And they were amazed and wondered, saying, "Are not all these who are speaking Galileans? And how is it that we hear, each of us in his own native language? Parthians and Medes and Elamites and residents of Mesopotamia, Judea and Cappadocia, Pontus and Asia, Phrygia and Pamphylia, Egypt and the parts of Libya belonging to Cyrene, and visitors from Rome, both Jews and proselytes, Cretans and Arabians, we hear them telling in our own tongues the mighty works of God." (Acts 2:6–11)

If you're going to read this paragraph on Pentecost, give yourself some research time beforehand to learn how to pronounce all those names—Phrygia, Pamphylia, Cyrene, and so on. Otherwise you'll feel foolish trying to sound them out for the first time in front of a couple hundred people. (Here's a hint: If you don't know, just bluster through as if you're perfectly confident. It's what I do.)

But the parade of names sure gets the point across. Suddenly these ignorant Galileans—fishermen and manual laborers and (ugh!) tax collectors—have dropped their accents. They can speak every language known to man. Or maybe it would be better to say that the people listening can *hear* every language known to man.

That's what the fire of the Spirit is doing for them: It's taking the message they have, which they could never in a million years figure out how to get across to all these people, and making it understandable to everyone from everywhere. It's burning away the things that stand between them and other people—the prejudices, the stereotypes, the hatred and petty jealousy. Suddenly they understand what Jesus meant when he said, "But you shall receive power when the Holy Spirit has come upon you; and you shall be my witnesses in Jerusalem and in all Judea and Samaria and to the end of the earth." (Acts 1:8)

> "And all were amazed and perplexed, saying to one another, 'What does this mean?' But others mocking said, 'They are filled with new wine.'" (Acts 2:12–13)

That little sarcastic joke probably passes right over our heads every time we hear it. Or if it doesn't, it probably makes us think only about the cynical mockers who said it, and how they just didn't get it. We shake our heads at them. Here's a miracle, right in front of their eyes, and all they can do is yawn and make snide remarks.

But now let's think for a moment about what it tells us about the apostles. They look like they're drunk! They're so ecstatic, so filled with joy, that their personalities have completely changed. One moment they're keeping to themselves, looking over their shoulders, locking the doors, hoping no one will notice them and take them off to be crucified like Jesus. The next moment, they're running out into the street, jumping up on tables, shouting their message to everyone who will listen.

From introverts to extroverts in thirty seconds!

When you think about it that way, it's easy to see why some people could think they were drunk. What else changes a person so quickly and so completely?

The ones who thought the apostles were drunk probably looked like the smart ones in the crowd. "

> But Peter, standing with the eleven, lifted up his voice and addressed them, 'Men of Judea and all who dwell in Jerusalem, let this be known to you, and give ear to my words. For these men are not drunk, as you suppose, since it is only the third hour of the day . . .'"
> (Acts 2:14–15)

Peter must have added that part because he knew that saying, "We would never, ever get drunk, honest!" wouldn't fly with this audience. Galilean fishermen? Yeah, drunk was usually a possibility. But not at nine o'clock in the morning!

> ". . . but this is what was spoken by the prophet Joel: 'And in the last days it shall be, God declares, that I will pour out my Spirit upon all flesh, and your sons and your daughters shall prophesy, and your young men shall see visions, and your old men shall dream dreams; yea, and on my menservants and my maidser-

vants in those days I will pour out my Spirit; and they
shall prophesy.'" (Acts 2:16–18)

This prophecy of the last days, Peter tells them, is coming true
now. (Incidentally, if you're keeping score at home, that must
mean that these are the "last days," right?)

You see what the prophecy from Joel tells us. There may
have been a time when only designated prophets and members
of the priestly caste could speak for God, but in the last days—
that's now—completely unimportant people will prophesy.
Did you notice how Joel said "sons and daughters"? "Menser-
vants and maidservants"? Women were not considered important in Jewish society (although they were considerably more
important than women in pagan society in those days).

But now even *those* from Galilee speak for God.

It really must be the last days.

• • • •

From here Peter goes on to give his audience an impromptu
tour of salvation history, right up to the crucifixion and resurrection of Jesus Christ. That crucifixion was very recent when
Peter was talking—just a few weeks before, in fact. And what
is Peter's message?

You killed God.

That's kind of a downer, isn't it?

If Peter had hired a consultant, he would have probably
been told that's not the way to appeal to an audience. You need
to emphasize the positive. "Hey, be nice to each other, and you
can be happy. It really works. Now let me tell you about the six
can't-miss habits of really well-adjusted people."

So it's a good thing Peter didn't hire a consultant, because what he said to the people there on that day was exactly what they needed to hear. It worked—he reached his target demographic perfectly.

> Now when they heard this they were cut to the heart, and said to Peter and the rest of the apostles, "Brethren, what shall we do?"

> And Peter said to them, "Repent, and be baptized every one of you in the name of Jesus Christ for the forgiveness of your sins; and you shall receive the gift of the Holy Spirit. For the promise is to you and to your children and to all that are far off, every one whom the Lord our God calls to him." And he testified with many other words and exhorted them, saying, "Save yourselves from this crooked generation."

> So those who received his word were baptized, and there were added that day about three thousand souls. (Acts 2:37–41)

Three thousand people baptized at once! Think about that for a while.

I've done a lot of parish missions. I've spoken all over the country. Let me tell you, if I ever had a day when I got three thousand non-Catholics to join the Catholic Church, I'd consider it a pretty successful day. I'd also probably go home and faint.

And I'm a professional speaker. I don't mean I'm the greatest there ever was, but I've spent a lot of time learning what works and what doesn't.

Peter was just some guy Jesus picked off a fishing boat among, you know, *those people.*

Just think of the logistics of getting three thousand people baptized. Think how long you'd have to wait in line if you were number 2,781. These weren't casual thrill seekers. They didn't say to themselves, "Well, why not? I could use a bath, and it's free." Most of them had to wait for hours—hours when they could have been thinking to themselves, "I don't know about this. I've got important stuff to do. I already had a bath last Friday." Something had to have moved them in a considerable way. Think about it: They had to put off all the things they'd planned on doing that day, break all their appointments, miss dinner with the family—all because of what Peter had said to them.

And why did they do it?

Probably because they had just lived through the most exciting thing that had ever happened in their lives.

They saw fireworks. They watched as working-class Galilean fishermen turned into world-class theologians. They heard the most amazing story from Peter that went right to their hearts.

Their lives had changed in a moment. And they never wanted to go back.

• • • •

Everything in the Christian community starts from that day, which is why we always think of Pentecost as the birthday of the Church.

Before Pentecost, the Christians were still in shock. Jesus had always been there, in the flesh, to tell them what to do. Then he was crucified, and that was horrible. Then he reappeared alive, and hundreds saw him giving the same account. And then he ascended into heaven.

That last part might even have been worse than the crucifixion. Jesus had left them. He wasn't taken away against his will—he actually went away, telling them they could continue the mission themselves.

What would they do now? Jesus had left his apostles in charge, and all they could do was sit around and pray. There's nothing wrong with sitting around and praying—in fact, we should all do a lot more of it. But it almost seems as though the apostles had lost the will to do anything else.

Then came Pentecost, and everything changed.

The rest of the Acts of the Apostles, from chapter 2 on, is the story of the apostles going out into the world and taking the message to anyone who will listen. They travel everywhere. They get into shipwrecks. They get thrown into prison. They get chased by angry mobs with pitchforks.

And absolutely nothing stops them.

Before they were quivering jelly, and now they're unstoppable!

What happened? The Holy Spirit came, and the apostles were set on fire.

• • • •

The Acts of the Apostles doesn't finish the story, for the very good reason that most of the apostles were still alive when Luke was writing his book.

So what happened after that?

We have to rely on tradition to tell us what became of the apostles. Some of the traditions are more reliable than others, but when we put them all together we get a clear overall picture. The apostles went everywhere and did everything. They had no fear. They knew they would succeed, even if they died while they were doing it. And they didn't worry at all about dying, because they had found something worth dying for.

That's the power of the Spirit at work.

Peter and Paul died together in Rome, as you already know—Peter by crucifixion (upside down, may I add), Paul by beheading. By that time they had brought tens of thousands into the Church.

James was the first of the Twelve Apostles to die—in fact, he is the only one whose death is recorded in the Bible: "About that time Herod the king laid violent hands upon some who belonged to the church. He killed James the brother of John with the sword; and when he saw that it pleased the Jews, he proceeded to arrest Peter also." (Acts 12:1–2) Peter, of course, escaped from prison, but James was executed, probably because he had fearlessly told the king exactly where he was wrong.

The other James, son of Alphaeus, was probably martyred while preaching the Gospel in Egypt.

Thomas—you remember, the doubter—went to India. That's what the traditions all say, both in the West and in India. Rome had an insatiable appetite for pepper from India, so there were hundreds of trading ships going back and forth between the Roman Empire and India every year. If Thomas wanted to go to India, all he had to do was hop aboard. There are hundreds of thousands of Christians in India today whose ancient traditions say that the apostle Thomas founded their Church, and we don't have any good reason not to believe them. The legends say that Thomas was martyred in India, but not before he had spent many years there preaching and converting thousands. Not bad for a man who refused to believe that Jesus was alive.

Nathanael, or Bartholomew (almost all of Jesus' friends had a Hebrew name and a Greek name), also went to India (or to Parthia; it was hard to tell where Parthia ended and India began). They say he was flayed alive after converting the King of Armenia, which was on the way back from India (or Parthia).

Judas "not Iscariot," the one we remember as Saint Jude, preached in Armenia with Bartholomew, and later ended up a martyr in Beirut.

Matthew spent a lot of his time preaching in Palestine, but he may have gone as far as Ethiopia.

Simon the Zealot traveled all over the Middle East, and the most common tradition says he was martyred in present-day Georgia (the country, not the American state).

Andrew, Peter's brother, spread the Gospel in Greece, and was ultimately crucified there. A very ancient tradition says that he also traveled as far as present Russia and Ukraine.

Philip preached in what is now Greece and Turkey.

Matthias, who replaced Judas as one of the Twelve, ended up in Ethiopia, according to a strong ancient tradition.

Finally, John lived a long life and grew to be so old that some Christians spread a strange rumor: He would not die until Jesus came.

> Peter turned and saw following them the disciple whom Jesus loved, who had lain close to his breast at the supper and had said, "Lord, who is it that is going to betray you?" When Peter saw him, he said to Jesus, "Lord, what about this man?"
>
> Jesus said to him, "If it is my will that he remain until I come, what is that to you? Follow me!"

> The saying spread abroad among the brethren that this
> disciple was not to die; yet Jesus did not say to him that
> he was not to die, but, "If it is my will that he remain
> until I come, what is that to you?" (John 21:20–23)

John did finally die at almost a hundred years old, apparently
of natural causes, after a long life of bold preaching in Ephesus.

These were the twelve men who sat cowering in Jerusalem
before Pentecost, hardly daring to go out in public. After Pentecost, each one of them became an unstoppable Gospel ma-
chine. Each one defied death to catch up with him—and when
it did, he faced it boldly, knowing that Christ was waiting for
him.

That's the fire of the Spirit at work, burning away fear and
doubt.

• • • •

The fire didn't go out after the first generation. Jesus promised
that he would always be with us, and he keeps his promises.

Think what the Church has accomplished.

For nearly three hundred years, it was *illegal* to be Christian. Not just illegal as in a fine of not less than fifty dollars,
or illegal as in a suspended driver's license, but illegal as in
thrown to the lions, crucified, beheaded, skinned alive, or
whatever else might amuse some local Roman official.

Yet in that time the Church grew and grew. If the Roman
government left the Christians alone for a while, the Church
grew. If the Roman government started torturing them to
death again, people saw how boldly the Christians faced death,
and the Church grew *faster*.

That's the fire of the Spirit at work.

By the time Constantine finally made Christianity legal in 312, the Christians were probably the single biggest religious group in the Roman Empire. There were hundreds of thousands of them, and millions just a few years later, willing to defy death because of what they knew was right!

That sounds like more than enthusiasm. That sounds like a miracle.

And all that time, the Christians weren't just thinking of themselves. They had plenty of problems, and it would have been easy for them to say, "Until the persecutions are over, we have to lie low and keep out of trouble."

But they never did that.

Jesus had told them that whatever they did for the poor and forgotten, they did for him.

So the Christians took care of the poor, the sick, the imprisoned. They took care of their own, of course, but they didn't stop there. They took care of everyone. They responded to the need first and asked questions later.

When epidemics came—and horrible epidemics swept through the Roman world every few years—the Christians insisted on taking care of the sick, even if they got sick and died themselves. (The pagan doctors were more likely to be out of town at the first sign of an outbreak, knowing what was coming and that their medicine couldn't do anything for it.) The Spirit that gave them courage to face the lions gave them the same courage to face the plagues.

And often that made the difference between death and life to the victim of the disease. If some kind Christian was there to bring water when he was thirsty, to give him basic comforts, and to keep his spirits up, a sick man might very well survive the plague. And what would he think of Christians when he recovered? He'd probably have a much better opinion of them. He might very well become a Christian himself.

Even the pagans had to admit that Christians took care of people when pagans didn't. After Christianity had been the favored religion of the empire for a while, the emperor Julian (history calls him Julian the Apostate) tried to push the empire back to paganism. But the only way he could imagine making it work was to imitate the Christians "by distributing from a little liberally to the needy, by giving with a willing mind, and by endeavoring to do as much good as possible." That was necessary, he said, because the "Galileans" (his would-be insulting name for the Christians) trapped people in their fiendish web by doing good.

Christians were like strangers with candy, Julian said. And what candy did they offer? Well, good works, charity, taking care of the poor and the sick, stuff like that. Crafty devils!

And even when he ordered his pagan priests to imitate Christian charity, Julian realized that it would never really happen unless the government paid for it. He made arrangements for payments from the government to take care of setting up hospitals, homes for the homeless, and other things that Christians were doing without any help from the government.

But guess what? That, too, died off. And the Christians were left doing what they've always done.

The institutions that care for the poor all over Europe started with the Catholic church. Here in America, there's a pretty high probability that the first hospital in your city was founded by the Catholic Church. Even where there are government programs to take care of the poor, the whole idea that the poor should be taken care of is, as Julian recognized, a Christian thing.

What makes us Christians do these things? It's the fire of the Spirit. It's God telling us, "Yes, you can." It's that burning away of every fear, every inhibition, everything that stands in our way.

And that's why if you want a life radically different from the rest, the only place to find it is in the Catholic Church.

7. SAINTS ALIVE

Do you know the story of Saint Leo the Great? He was pope at a time when things were pretty bad for Rome. The empire was falling apart. One barbarian horde after another came rampaging across the landscape. And worst of them all was Attila the Hun.

You've probably heard of Attila the Hun, because even after more than a millennium and a half, his name is still synonymous with "unstoppable barbarian horror." He destroyed cities one after another as his Huns surged across the empire from right to left and back again. And now he had the city of Rome in his sights. He was headed south through Italy, still leveling cities as completely as if he had nuclear weapons. Some of them would never be rebuilt. The Roman army had given up. The people of Rome were in a panic.

They turned to the only leader they trusted: their bishop, Leo.

But what could a bishop do against the most destructive army in history?

He couldn't lead soldiers out to fight, because there were no soldiers left. A militia of the Roman citizens at this point would be a rabble of doddering retirees and little old ladies. The Huns covered the ground like locusts wherever they went.

So what did Leo do? He went out to meet Attila.

He didn't take an army with him. He just went out un-armed and asked to talk to Attila in private for a while. And when he was done, Attila turned around and went away.

What did the bishop say? Nobody knows. But whatever it was, it sure worked.

Now, I think that's just about the most exciting war story I've ever heard. Forget all the battles against impossible odds. Forget all your favorite John Wayne movies (that's going to be difficult for my mother to do). Here's a single man who goes out against the most horrible—and successful—conqueror the world has ever known, and he doesn't even carry a Nerf bat.

And he wins! That's completely amazing to me. Attila is armed to the teeth. He's got a hundred thousand or more Huns behind him, and they're all armed to the teeth, too. And here comes Leo, a guy in a bishop's robe. Talk about impossible odds.

But it's Attila who blinks.

This is what you're in for when you get to know the saints. You'll hear amazing stories of courage and rip-roaring ad-venture, of love and almost superhuman devotion. Above all, you'll see absolute fearlessness.

After all, fear is boring.

• • • •

One of the great things about getting to know the saints is that you're not just hearing stories—although they're great stories, and I don't want to diminish the power of a great story. You're making friends—real friends, not imaginary friends, because the saints are very much alive, and they actually do care about us.

That's what we mean when we talk about the "communion of saints" in the creed. God's people on earth and God's people in heaven—we're all connected. The saints really are watching over us.

Ask for their help. They'll pray for you, and God listens to them.

That's why we Catholics make such a big deal of the saints. They're our friends, and they're the kind of friends who come through when you really need them. So we Catholics often pick favorite saints, people whose lives really inspire us. And on important occasions, we like to remember those favorite saints.

• • • •

Getting married is one of the most important things a Catholic will ever do. It's not just some arrangement that you and your partner make for your personal convenience. It's a *vocation*—the way you live out the mission God has given you, the way in which he desires to save your soul. Some people are called to be priests or bishops, and some are called to be monks or nuns. But many are called to be married.

Don't think you're not serving God just because you're not a nun or a priest. God wants you, and if you're married, God has decided that's how he needs you to serve him.

Now, I bring all this up because when my wife, Teresa, and I were married, we wanted to make a sort of statement about our vocation (no, not with chair covers). We decided to get married on the feast of Saint Augustine.

Why Augustine? Well, for a lot of reasons. But mostly because he's one of the most exciting characters in history.

We know more about Saint Augustine than we know about practically any other human being in the ancient world. Why? Because he told us himself.

Saint Augustine invented the autobiography. There are other ancient people who wrote books about themselves—Nehemiah, for example, and Julius Caesar. But they stuck mostly to the facts that anyone could see from the outside. What makes Augustine so different is that he turned himself inside out and showed us what was in his soul. Not just the good things, either. In fact, not even mostly the good things. Augustine told us practically every important sin he had ever committed from the time he was a baby—literally.

> Bit by bit I began to perceive where I was, and I wanted to declare my desires to those who might satisfy them, and I could not; for my desires were inside me, and they were outside me, nor could any one of their senses enter into my soul. Therefore I made motions and sounds as signs to express my wants, the few that I could, and such as I could, for they had very little resemblance with what I would express; and when my will was not complied with, either because I was not understood, or because what I desired was hurtful, I was angry that my elders would not be subject to me, and that they who are free would not be my slaves, and I took my revenge upon them by crying. Such have I found other infants to be; and that I was such, those infants without knowing what they were doing have better informed me than the knowledge of my nurses.[2]

You've seen some tell-all autobiographies, I'm sure, but how many of those writers confess the sins they committed when they were babies? I mean, come on, he was just a baby—is it really wrong for babies to cry? But Augustine is tracing sin to its roots, and he finds that as a baby he was selfish, angry, and vengeful. And you know what? He's right. That's what original sin means, isn't it? We're born sinners.

This is a different kind of excitement. With Leo the Great, we had a story of adventure, a lone man against impossible odds. With Augustine, we have the kind of excitement you get when your brain has just grown three sizes. Suddenly things make sense that never made sense before.

But the one thing they have in common is total fearlessness. Nothing would stop Leo from going out to meet Attila, even though Attila had a reputation for amusing himself by torturing Romans to death. Augustine would tell us every sin he could think of, not caring what it might do to his reputation. Both of them acted without fear. That doesn't necessarily mean they never *felt* fear—in fact, Augustine will tell you quite clearly how much he worried about his own reputation. But it means they were able to overcome their fears and do what had to be done, because ultimately they trusted in the power of the Spirit.

I can't tell you how many people I've known who've lived lives just like Augustine's. He grew up with a good Catholic mother, whom we know today as Saint Monica. But he went away to college and got to know a bunch of intellectual types. Like college kids everywhere, they thought they knew everything. And like a million nice Catholic kids today, Augustine let himself be swayed by his "intellectual" friends. He thought he was way smarter than his mother. He wasn't going to fall for that old-fashioned Catholic stuff.

So he tried all sorts of trendy philosophies. You can imagine him sitting around with the other trendy intellectuals in black berets, smoking clove cigarettes and rattling off big philosophical terms as if they knew what they meant.

Of course, one of the things these bright college kids knew all about was sex. It's amazing, isn't it, how when you're that age, your generation is the first to discover sex? I mean, how did people get by all those thousands of years before you, when they didn't understand it?

So Augustine fell right in with their thinking, and went looking for all the sex he could find. Eventually he ended up living with his girlfriend. He got her pregnant (who would have thought that could happen?), and they had a son—but they still didn't get married.

Meanwhile, like any good Catholic mother, Monica worried about her son. She was proud of him, of course. He was turning into one of the top intellectuals of the age. But that wasn't good enough for Monica. "Please, God," she prayed, "just let me live long enough to see my son come back to the Catholic Church."

You know, prayer is a powerful thing. And I don't think there's anything more powerful than the prayer of a Catholic mother. Nothing Monica could say would make her son turn away from his trendy philosophy of the moment and come back to the Catholic Church. But God heard her prayers and sent the one thing that could help: a man who was a towering intellectual, one of the greatest minds of the age—and also a Catholic bishop.

Ambrose was the Bishop of Milan (I'm proud to say in Des Moines our cathedral is named after him), where Augustine went to take a teaching job. At that time Milan was a more prosperous city even than Rome, so the job was a big deal. Ambrose saw that the young Augustine had a keen mind, so he took time out of his busy schedule just to be Augustine's friend. They talked about everything, and Augustine came to see that yes, maybe some of the smartest people in the world were Catholics.

And it worked. Augustine began to feel deeply sorry for the way he had wasted his life. He started to think that God could never forgive him for all his sins. He wasn't quite converted yet, but he had seen that he needed something he didn't have. He prayed over and over, begging God not to be angry with him—but he couldn't get over the feeling that he was unworthy.

> "And you, O Lord, how long? How long, O Lord? Will you be angry to the end? Be not mindful of our old iniquities"—for I perceived myself to be held by them. And I threw out lamentable complaints. "How long? How long? Tomorrow and tomorrow! Why not now? Why not this very hour an end to my filthiness?"
>
> I spoke these things, and I wept with a most bitter contrition of my heart. And suddenly I heard a voice from a neighboring house, as of a boy or a girl, I don't know which, saying in a sing-song voice, over and over, *Tolle lege, tolle lege*—"pick up and read, pick up and read."[3]

Do children usually run around singing "Pick up and read"? Augustine didn't think they did. Maybe it was the message from God he'd been waiting for. He picked up the book of Romans, which happened to be sitting in the next room, and read from the first passage he came to:

> ". . . not in reveling and drunkenness, not in debauchery and licentiousness, not in quarreling and jealousy. But put on the Lord Jesus Christ, and make no pro-

vision for the flesh, to gratify its desires." (Romans 13:13–14)

"I would read no further," Augustine tells us, "nor was there need: for with the end of this sentence, it was as if a light of confidence and security had streamed into my heart. All the darkness of my former hesitation was dispelled."[4]

Next to Saint Paul's, this is possibly the most famous conversion story in the world. It has inspired countless millions of Christians. Countless millions of non-Christians have read Augustine's *Confessions,* too—it's one of the fundamental works of European literature—and no one knows how many of them have been converted themselves as they read.

None of that would have been possible without Augustine's complete fearlessness. After his conversion, he went on to become one of the most famous theologians of his time—probably of all time. He was made Bishop of Hippo, an important city in the Roman province of Africa, and even in his own lifetime everyone read his books.

That's quite a reputation to put in jeopardy by telling the world what a rotten kid you were in your twenties.

I remember the first time I read Augustine's *Confessions.* I wanted to know what kind of man could put his mother through everything Monica had to go through. But by the end of the book I knew the answer: a saint.

You see, a saint isn't someone who's led a perfect life. A saint is someone who, at the right moment, found the power of the Holy Spirit. With the fire of the Spirit, you can burn through all your fears and be *free*.

"Free" doesn't mean being able to do whatever you want whenever you want to do it. That actually would make you a slave to your whims, your passions—whatever you want to call them. No, to be free, you have to be willing to follow what is good, what is virtuous. And what the saints have discovered is that you can be free to do what's right even if someone is standing right there waiting to kill you for doing it. The only thing that stops you is fear. Take that away and you're free. And that's what the fire of the Spirit does: It burns away the fear.

By now, you're seeing the pattern.

• • • •

I think when a lot of people consider saints, they think first of the martyrs. I purposely didn't start out with martyrs, because I didn't want to suggest that you have to get yourself killed to be a saint. Leo, Augustine, Ambrose, and Monica were all saints, and they all died of natural causes.

But still, if you want to talk about fearlessness, it's hard to get more fearless than the martyrs. (Although I sometimes think I'd *rather* die than open up my whole interior life the way Augustine did.)

Think about what it took to be a Christian in the first three hundred years of the Church. Remember that it was illegal to be Christian—not pay-a-fine illegal, but thrown-to-the-lions illegal. Yet there were millions of Christians by the time Constantine finally made the religion legal in 312.

They were mostly ordinary people—bakers and shoe salesmen, people who had to work for a living. They had families to support and bills to worry about, just like you and I do.

But when the persecution came, thousands of them were willing to die rather than give up their faith.

We have the diary of one of those ordinary people, a young mother named Perpetua. She had a lot to live for—a son who was only a year or two old, and a father who loved her and begged her to give up this Christian nonsense. And it would have been very easy to do what they asked of her. All she had to do was offer a pinch of incense to the pagan gods and she would be free. But she refused.

Her story shows what Christians sometimes have had to face—not just their own death, but the pleas of their loved ones and the glare of publicity. You need a lot of courage to stand up to those.

After a few days there prevailed a report that we should be heard. And then my father came to me from the city, worn out with anxiety. He came up to me, that he might cast me down, saying, "Have pity, my daughter, on my grey hairs. Have pity on your father, if I am worthy to be called a father by you. If with these hands I have brought you up to this flower of your age, if I have preferred you to all your brothers, do not deliver me up to the scorn of men. Have regard to your brothers, have regard to your mother and your aunt, have regard to your son, who will not be able to live after you. Lay aside your courage, and do not bring us all to destruction; for none of us will speak in freedom if you should suffer anything."

These things said my father in his affection, kissing my hands, and throwing himself at my feet; and with tears he called me not Daughter, but Lady. And I grieved over the grey hairs of my father, that he alone of all my family would not rejoice over my passion. And I comforted him, saying, "On that scaffold whatever God wills shall happen. For know that we are not placed in our own power, but in that of God."

And he departed from me in sorrow. [5]

Like tyrants everywhere, the Roman judge thought he could change Perpetua's mind by torturing her innocent family. But Perpetua was strong. She had the fire of the Spirit in her, and it burned up her fear and doubt. That doesn't mean she didn't grieve for her family (although, as it turned out, her son was able to survive her), but she saw that what was really important was the truth, and she had the strength to hold fast to that truth even when it meant death.

• • • •

Well, that all happened a long time ago. I think some people have the mistaken impression that all the saints are people who lived long ago. That's partly because some of the old-time saints are very popular. And they should be. Saint Augustine is one of the most amazing characters in history. It doesn't matter whether he lived on earth a millennium and a half ago or last week. And he's still alive, and always will be.

But there are also plenty of more recent saints.

In fact, there are probably more saints alive right now than there ever have been at any time in the past. A saint, after all, is anyone who's made it into heaven. I don't know how many people are going to heaven, but I hope it's a lot. And there are more Christians alive now than there ever have been before. It just stands to reason that a lot of them will be saints.

We use the word saint in two ways, though. When we commonly speak of the saints, we mean the people the Church has officially recognized as such. That doesn't mean there aren't millions or billions of others, but when the Church adds a saint to the calendar, it means that we've done some extraordinarily thorough research into that person's life. That kind of research takes some time.

Still, there have been more saints recognized in the past century than at any other time in history. Under Pope John Paul II, more saints were canonized than in the five hundred years before him—and a lot of those people lived quite recently. The twentieth century had Nazis and decades of Communist oppression, but those are exactly the conditions that produce saints. The fire of the Spirit comes just when we need it most.

Think of Saint Maximilian Kolbe, for example. He was martyred by Nazis, who were every bit as ruthless as those Romans who used to throw Christians to the lions. Like most Polish intellectuals, he was sent to a concentration camp. One day three prisoners escaped, and the Nazis decided it would discourage future escape attempts if they killed ten prisoners in their place . Once you decide that human life is worthless, you can make ridiculous decisions like that.

So the Nazis picked ten men at random to be sent to the starvation chamber. When one of the men begged for his life on the grounds that he had a family, Maximilian said, "Send me instead."

"Who are you?" the guards asked.

"I'm a priest," he answered. He had no family to worry about, so he would take the other man's place. And the Nazi guards didn't care much who died, as long as they had ten dead bodies at the end of the process. So they took the priest and left the other man.

The men were locked in a room and left to starve. Kolbe prayed with them and encouraged them, reminding them that they'd soon be out of reach of the Nazis in heaven. Every time the guards looked into the cell, Kolbe was on his knees, praying or singing hymns. One by one the others died, until only

Kolbe was left alive. Eventually the guards were tired of waiting to clear out the cell and killed him by lethal injection.

But the man whose place he took, Franciszek Gajownic-
zek, survived the camp. And he never stopped telling the story
of the priest who had given up his life for him. In fact, Gaj-
owniczek lived to be ninety-three—long enough to be Pope
John Paul II's guest at the Vatican when Maximilian Kolbe
was canonized as a saint.

And speaking of John Paul II, there's another saint with an
amazingly exciting life. He lived through the Second World
War, too, studying to be a priest in a secret seminary while the
Nazis occupied Poland, hiding in basements while Nazi thugs
searched for him, helping Jewish neighbors escape whenever
he could.

The world was amazed when this Polish archbishop was
elected pope. It was the first time anyone from outside Italy
had been pope. And while the world was amazed, the Communist governments were terrified. What would it mean to
have a pope from Communist Poland?

"Do not be afraid." That was John Paul's message to the
people of Poland and the whole world. And they took it to
heart. Poland had always been a trouble spot for the Communist empire in Eastern Europe. Now, with a Polish pope, it
seemed as if anything was possible.

And you know the rest of the story. John Paul was one of the
most traveled leaders in world history. The Communists tried
to have him assassinated, but it didn't work. John Paul lived
to see the entire Communist establishment crumble across Europe—starting, of course, with Poland. And even among the
Communists, there were many who said that the collapse happened for one simple reason: John Paul II told the people, "Do
not be afraid."

That's the fire of the Spirit at work. It spreads out from one remarkable man and burns away the fear in whole countries.

So there's another modern saint I don't think of as boring. I think if you bring down all the governments in Eastern Europe, you've done something pretty exciting. People are already starting to call him John Paul the Great—just like old Pope Leo the Great, who stared down Attila the Hun and made him blink.

I'm also obsessed (in a good way, of course) with Mother Teresa—officially, Blessed Teresa of Calcutta. Who was she? A frail little old lady. I remember seeing a picture of her with President and Mrs. Reagan. Nancy Reagan towered over her, and Nancy is five feet four. Yet Mother Teresa is the powerful one in that picture. I mean, sure, Ronald Reagan could push the nuclear button whenever he felt like it, and Nancy Reagan got to hobnob with all the leaders of the world. But you get the feeling that they posed for this picture because they wanted people to know they met Mother Teresa. You don't get the feeling that Mother Teresa needed everybody to know that she met the Reagans. I say that makes her the powerful one.

Mother Teresa was actually Albanian, but we think of her as Teresa of Calcutta because she spent most of her life in India. Why? Because she found people who needed her there. She became a citizen of India in 1948, and she spent her whole life among the poorest of the poor, helping the sick and the dying. Just the smell, frankly, would have turned most people away. But she inspired others to the point where she ended up founding her own order of hardworking nuns. While other orders, who lived like modern businesswomen, saw their numbers dwindling away, Mother Teresa's Missionaries of Charity kept growing and growing, though they spent their lives in the stench of the poorest areas of Calcutta and other parts of the world where people were in desperate need. Why did these women want to go into the parts of the world that were most unpleasant and spend their lives helping the helpless?

I think it's because doing the "same old, same old" just wasn't exciting for them. But picking up your cross and following Jesus to places in the world that are anything but comfortable was.

And what about now? How many people currently living will be recognized as saints a hundred years from now? How many of them will be remembered in statues and stained-glass windows?

I think there are a lot of those people alive right now, because the fire of the Spirit comes just when we need it most. And right now, I think we really need it.

8. WHAT'S WRONG WITH THE WORLD

What's wrong with the world today?

I'm sure you have a list. And your list is probably different from mine. But we'd all probably start with one or two of the seven deadly sins.

So why is there so much wrong with the world?

That's a hard question. But, as it happens, I think I have an easy answer.

I think the world is looking for love.

I don't mean the kind of "love" portrayed in pop culture. I don't think the world is looking for another planet to hold hands around. I mean the kind of love I wrote about at the beginning of this book: God's love, one in which we give ourselves away.

The trouble is that the world doesn't know it's looking for God's love. We know there's something missing, and we keep looking for things to fill that hole.

So we see pornography everywhere, trails of broken families, lives derailed by alcohol and drug addiction, politicians scrambling for power, and so on and so on. And unfortunately, we often find ourselves at the center of it. But deep down, we know it's not working. The publishing industry has known for a long time now that you really can't go wrong selling self-help books. We snap them up by the millions—magazines, too. The next time you're standing in line at the supermarket checkout, count how many magazine articles there are—just the ones advertised on the covers—that promise to fix your deepest personal problems. You're not happy? Here are forty-seven things you must do to fix what's wrong with you. It's always a numbered list, because people pay attention to numbered lists. That's nothing new. Remember that we have the Ten Commandments. Although, for some reason, you don't usually see those on magazine covers at the supermarket checkout.

So we have a whole industry devoted to helping us fix what's wrong with us. But you know what? It doesn't get fixed. Whatever it is, it's still wrong. So we buy another book, pick up another magazine, watch another TV show that promises to reveal the secret to contentment. They all promise to help us discover happiness and hope.

But not a single one has given us the answer we are looking for.

So we have terrible vices that aren't working for us, and even-well intentioned advice isn't doing the trick.

Where do we turn?

• • • •

Selfishness is boring.

Let me bare my soul to you for a minute and you'll see why.

I was scared to death when Teresa and I found out she was pregnant. Sure, we knew it was only a matter of time. And we also knew we wanted a big family. But that was just all in our minds. It's completely different when the reality of your conversations and dreams enters the womb for the first time. I couldn't help but think that from the beginning of time this child would be entrusted to me and Teresa to get to heaven. I still get anxious just thinking about it, and he's almost two.

I wasn't nervous because I didn't think we could take care of him. After all, he's the first grandchild on both sides—the kid is well taken care of. I was nervous because life as I knew it was about to disappear.

See, I said things that I think are pretty normal for first-time parents. Things like, "When will I have time for *me?*" And, "Is it even possible to function on three hours of sleep?" You probably understand the fear, too. We don't like giving up control. We don't want to have responsibilities. All human beings, including me, can be pretty selfish.

But what I've found after getting married to Teresa and having Joseph has been astonishing. I've found that I'm at my best only when they are.

We're taught that the way to be happy is to get, get, get. But now I can't imagine things differently. I can't imagine a life in which I don't have them to love! I remember what my life was like before, and it was great, but it was nowhere near the joy I have now. I'm a happier man.

• • • •

Do you know what the divorce rate in America is these days?

Nobody really does. It's a more complicated question than it seems, because as soon as you ask how likely it is that a couple getting married today will get divorced, you have to make a bunch of assumptions about the future that you can never prove.

But a good estimate is that nearly half of all marriages end in divorce.

Nearly half!

I'm sure you've probably heard that before, but that doesn't mean it gets any easier each time we hear it. Now, call me the eternal optimist or whatever, but I think this problem can be solved. Not because I came up with any answers—believe me, I didn't—but because Jesus did.

I want you to think back to your wedding day, if you're married. Or think about what you want your wedding to be like, if you're not married yet. What kind of promises do people make at weddings?

I know it's really fashionable to write your own vows these days, but Catholics don't usually do that. We think of marriage as a sacrament, so we don't leave the vows to chance. We do have different options for the vows, but they all make sure to remind us that we're in this for life. One form gets quite explicit: "for better, for worse, for richer, for poorer, in sickness and in health, until death do us part."

We put those words in the vows for a reason. If you're always asking, "What am I getting out of this marriage?" then you'll never get anything out of it. It's only when you concentrate on the complete giving of self that the marriage becomes really exciting. I've seen this manifest itself in some pretty awesome couples today. And Teresa and I stay close to them.

Selfishness is boring.

Think what a miserable existence it is to be looking constantly at your marriage and thinking, "I could do better." You're sitting at breakfast with your wife, and you're thinking, "I could do better." You're out at an expensive restaurant with your husband, and you're thinking, "I could do better." You're on vacation at the beach, and you're looking at each other, both of you thinking, "I could do better."

Look what you're doing! You're throwing away priceless moments of joy. You could be saying to yourself, "This is paradise! I'm with the one person I love most in the world, and we're doing something delightful together."

Instead, many today are saying, "I'm not happy *enough*. I'm not getting as much as I deserve. I want more." And because of that, many aren't happy at all.

In my previous book, *Mission of the Family,* I spent a long time talking about the fifth chapter of Ephesians. That's the one we frequently read at weddings, and it's the one that some people get mad about, because it tells wives to "be subject" to their husbands. And if it stopped there, I could probably understand why. But it doesn't at all.

> Husbands, love your wives, as Christ loved the church and gave himself up for her, that he might sanctify her, having cleansed her by the washing of water with the word, that he might present the church to himself in splendor, without spot or wrinkle or any such thing, that she might be holy and without blemish. Even so husbands should love their wives as their own bodies. He who loves his wife loves himself. For no man ever hates his own flesh, but nourishes and cherishes it, as Christ does the church, because we are members of his body. "For this reason a man shall leave his father and mother and be joined to his wife, and the two shall become one flesh." This mystery is a profound one, and I am saying that it refers to Christ and the church; however, let each one of you love his wife as himself, and let the wife see that she respects her husband. (Ephesians 5:15–33)

The husband is supposed to love his wife the way Christ loved the Church. Whenever Teresa thinks I'm not being quite the husband I should be, she always pulls that verse out and waves it in front of me. It's the trump card: "You're supposed to die for me."

She knows enough to realize that's not just to be taken in the literal sense (the literal might even be easier compared to what's coming). She knows that what Paul is speaking about is death in *everything,* in which I lay down my life completely for her, and she for me. That's what makes love worthwhile: total self-giving. I'm not saying I'm a perfect husband. I'm not saying I'm even a very good husband. But I see what the world offers, and I see what Christ offers—and I want Christ.

I'm going to tell you a true story. There was once a beautiful, smart, funny, friendly, successful woman who had a fiancé. She seemed like she had everything: a great job, an expensive car, a house of her own. She'd been married three times before, and she was about to get married for the fourth time. She always used to remind her third husband, and everyone else, that she could toss him in the Dumpster if she didn't think the marriage was working out the way she wanted. But now everything seemed bright: She said that this fiancé, the soon-to-be fourth husband, was everything the other three hadn't been.

Just weeks before the wedding, her fiancé came home and found her dead. She had killed herself.

It seems that she hadn't found what she wanted after all. And she wanted it so desperately that she couldn't live without it.

What was she looking for?

I don't know. I can't ask her.

But when I think about it, she had based her whole life on what she wanted. If she didn't get what she wanted out of a husband, she got rid of him and found a new one. Her house was always just the way she wanted it, and it was hers, even when she was living in it with the third husband. It was filled with things that cost a lot of money. Her car was expensive and flashy. She had possessions, including husbands, but possessions are nothing to live for.

Selfishness is boring. In her case, I think it just became unbearably boring.

• • • •

So, many of us have got a big hole in our lives we're trying to fill. And as I've made pretty clear, I think all those things are symptoms of the same problem.

We try to pound money, and status, and self-indulgence, and whatever else into that hole. But none of those things fit. They seem exciting for a while, but selfish indulgence is the wrong shape to fit into the hole. Because what we're looking for is something exciting to make our lives worthwhile, and—here's that dirty little secret again that no one tells you in our pop culture—selfishness is boring.

Now, why do I keep repeating this? After all, what I want for myself is all the things I enjoy. I want sex, money, fast cars, a big house, money, status, respect, and—while I'm at it—more money. How could life possibly be boring if I had everything I wanted?

Think about it for a while. What happens when your life is all about *you*?

I'm sure you've sat through a presentation, or a lecture, or a concert, where the microphone got too close to the loudspeaker. Suddenly you heard a high-pitched squeal that made all the people in the room cover their ears. That's what audio engineers call *feedback*.

Feedback happens when the signal comes out the speaker and goes in the microphone, gets amplified, and comes out the speaker and goes in the microphone, gets amplified, and comes out the speaker and goes in . . .

Well, you get the idea.

No one likes to hear feedback like that. It's loud, it's painful, and it's monotonous. And it completely cuts out any other sounds that might actually be interesting.

That's exactly what happens when your life is all about you. As Pope Francis says, you turn in on yourself. You care less and less about what's going on outside your own mind. You push away all the interesting stuff and focus only on yourself. Eventually, you're just the human equivalent of a high-pitched squeal. You hate your life. Why? Because you've cut out everything that might actually be interesting. You've cut out God's love.

When our lives become about only us, we have nothing to live for. But when we put away that selfishness, we start to see what really makes life worth living.

Selfishness is boring. Love, on the other hand—*God's love*—is the most attractive thing in the world.

• • • •

I'm happily married. But that doesn't mean that I never have difficulties in my marriage. We have arguments, disagreements, and all the little imperfections that come up in any human relationship. I'm sure you had arguments with your parents when you were growing up—but at the end of it all, they were still your parents.

Now, I'm going to tell you a little secret that you must never tell my wife: Most of these quarrels are my fault. Yes, she takes the blame and apologizes as often as I do, but I'm the one who really started it about 80 percent of the time. And it's almost always because of my selfishness.

(I was just kidding about not telling my wife, of course. Teresa already knows.)

Selfishness really doesn't work in marriage and it certainly doesn't work anywhere else. In fact, I think selfishness is what lies at the root of all our problems. The cure for selfishness is pretty obvious, and it's what Jesus preached about from the beginning: *mission.*

You see, as Catholics we don't simply believe we all are on a mission. Life isn't some Tom Cruise movie. Catholics believe we are mission. It's the foundation of who we are. And that mission is to be the light of the world. Think of it this way: Light is light. Light's mission is not to light up a room, but simply to be what it is: light. Now, the *effect* is that it lights up the room and our streets and so on, but it can only do those things because of what it is. Whew. (Read that sentence again and it will click.)

Selfishness is boring. And boredom makes us miserable. In extreme cases it makes us insane. So discover the mission of Jesus and do something interesting for a change.

We Catholics have a tradition of giving something up for Lent. It's a way of training ourselves for holiness, so to speak— reminding ourselves that indulging in petty pleasures (even chocolate) isn't the route to true happiness.

So typically when I ask people what they're giving up for Lent, I hear a list of the usual suspects. One person gives up chocolate. Another gives up meat. Another gives up beer and wine.

But I'll never forget the one Lent when I asked one of my friends what she was giving up, and she answered, "My mirror."

"Splendid!" I said (it's the only word that came to mind). If your appearance means so much to you that you spend more time looking in the mirror than lighting the world on fire with Christ's love, then maybe you should try giving up your mirror, too. Give yourself a chance to be who you were created to be!

You might be surprised by how happy you'll be.

I began this book by asking you a question: What do you dream of when you dream of happiness?

Maybe your first response was to think of all the nice things you don't have—a mansion, a limousine, a private jet, a tropical island of your own.

The trouble is that you're not likely to win the lottery. It could happen, theoretically, but it won't. I say that as confidently as I say that you won't get hit by a comet tomorrow. (If you *do* get hit by a comet tomorrow, bring this book back to me the next day and I'll give you your money back.)

So all those things you dreamt of are not likely to come your way. You can't have them. And if you think they're what will make you happy, then you're making yourself miserable.

But now that you've been reading for a while, maybe you have a better idea of happiness. Maybe you've learned that happiness is something literally anybody can have.

If you have, then you've learned the secret of the saints. You've learned what love really is.

Love isn't a soft-focus dream of running in slow motion through a field of daisies. Love isn't just sitting back and letting fuzzy feelings wash over you. Love is action. Love is mission.

And that's what the saints found—the kind of love that's always living and always exciting, a love in which we get out of the way and exhaust ourselves as disciples of the Lord Jesus Christ and his Church.

• • • •

Think about the saints again. Why are there cities all over the world named after saints?

The biggest city in South America is São Paulo, named after Saint Paul.

San Francisco is, obviously, named after Saint Francis. (And the other big city in California, Los Angeles, is named after the angels.) The capital of Costa Rica is San José. The full name of the Bolivian city La Paz is Nuestra Señora de La Paz—Our Lady of Peace. The capital of Paraguay is Asunción—short for Nuestra Señora Santa María de la Asunción, Our Lady Saint Mary of the Assumption.

You find these saints wherever you go. Go north—the capital of Newfoundland is St. John's, and the biggest city in New Brunswick is Saint John. (That always confuses geography students in Canada.) Go south—the oldest city in Florida, and in the continental United States, is St. Augustine, and the original colonial capital of Texas is San Antonio. Cross the water—the capital of Puerto Rico is San Juan.

And while we're there, how many islands in the Caribbean are named after saints? Saint Vincent, Saint Martin, Saint Barthélemy, Saint Eustatius, Saint Giles, Saint John, Saint Thomas—those are just the ones I can come up with.

I could go on and on with saint names. They're on our street signs. They're on our hospitals. They're on our mountains.

Why are we so obsessed with saints?

I think it's because they just amaze us. We don't understand what we want ourselves. But we look at them and we say, "Those people got it." We see how they lived their lives, and we think, "If only I could be like that." And you can!

You probably can't be like the playboy billionaire who flies to Monte Carlo for a weekend in his private Gulfstream jet. If you think that's what's going to make you happy, you obviously haven't seen any supermarket tabloids lately.

But you can be like Saint Augustine, who opened his heart to the world and showed us what was inside it. You can be like Mother Teresa, who gave her life to the poor. You can do these things, because they don't take money or status or any of the things you may not have. All they take is grace. And if you really pray for it, God will give it to you.

I'm not saying it will be easy or painless. And I'm not saying all your problems will go away. Love hurts sometimes.

Think of Mother Teresa again. She spent her life doing hard work, harder than most of us can imagine doing. And she did it in spite of the fact that she sometimes went for years without feeling the presence of God in her life. What sustained her was faith and love—faith that God would be there for her, even when she didn't feel it, and love for God, and for his people, who are the image of God.

Why do you still love your wife or your children or your mother when they're sick? They're a lot of trouble then, aren't they? But you love them anyway, and you'll take care of them no matter how hard it gets, because loving is just better than not loving. Yes, love can hurt. Yes, it might be easier not to feel anything at all.

But who wants to live that *way?*

The pain is worthwhile because it's the only route to the joy. There's no light without darkness, no joy without sorrow, no Easter without Good Friday.

That's why I think popular culture is all wrong—and the Catholic Church is completely right.

• • • •

You've heard enough from me by now to know that I'm a Catholic with a capital C. I'm all in on the faith. Not because I'm a "blind follower," but because I believe Jesus when he said to his missionaries, "He who hears you hears me, and he who rejects you rejects me, and he who rejects me rejects him who sent me." (Luke 10:16) I believe him when he said, "And I tell you, you are Peter, and on this rock I will build my church, and the powers of death shall not prevail against it." (Matthew 16:18)

If I didn't believe Jesus, I wouldn't be Catholic. That doesn't mean I get everything I want. Nor does it mean my life isn't a mess.

But what it does mean is I truly believe that the Church has the key to what life is all about—because she has Jesus.

So what do you think is wrong with the world now? I know there are people who will tell you that the Church is what's wrong. Pop culture shows us the Catholic Church as a bunch of miserable old men in a faraway land imposing out-of-touch teachings on the rest of us.

But that's not the Church.

We are the Church. Some may have more God-given authority than others, in the inverted-pyramid scheme that makes the pope "servant of the servants of God."

But the Church is *all* of us together. And as a group, all together, we show the rest of the world what Catholicism is really like. So how are you doing with it?

Honestly, I'm bored with the culture's take on the Church. I'm bored with the culture's take, period. Pop culture thinks all I care about is the same stories of celebrity divorce and who's wearing what, recycled over and over with different names. I want something fresh, something new. I want Jesus.

"And he who sat upon the throne said, 'Behold, I make all things new.'" (Revelation 21:5)

Without Jesus, it's the same old thing.

With Jesus, the world is new every day.

That's the secret of the saints. That's why Mother Teresa persuaded people to go into the worst parts of the world to help the sick and the dying. In the posh suburbs, it's the same old thing. But when you're doing Jesus' work, it's an adventure every hour of every day.

You see, I don't think I'm the only one who's bored with pop culture's take. I think even the people who are most immersed in pop culture are bored with it—look at what's going on with it. It always demands more and worse. We need everything to be bigger and louder. We need more vulgar language, more deviant sex, more gruesome violence. What was shocking last year is just ho-hum now, and it's because none of those things are really interesting. They're certainly not joyful.

Things that shock us the way pop culture does are just like drugs—we need a bigger and bigger fix to get high. It's not soul-stirring excitement; it's just a slap in the face. You feel it, and maybe it wakes you up, but it doesn't stir your soul.

But what we're looking for is joy. And the saints know where to find it. They know the secret our pop culture hasn't figured out: Joy is not boring. We keep hoping we'll find joy by getting more—more money, more power, more fame, more stuff. But none of those things bring us joy.

What brings us joy is complete self-giving. It can be painful, too, but you can't have real joy without it. It really is better to give than to receive. Jesus knew a thing or two about human nature. When he gave us the Sermon on the Mount, he wasn't just telling us, "Do these things and you'll make me happy." Rather, the whole point was to show us how to be happy ourselves.

So if we know what it takes to be happy, then shouldn't we be doing it?

And shouldn't the world see us doing it? Shouldn't people look at the Catholic Church and say, "Wow, those are the happiest people I've ever seen"?

Why isn't that happening?

I think it's because we're afraid. Though happiness is the one thing we want most, the whole goal of life, I think we're afraid to go after it.

9. BE NOT AFRAID

What's the one thing an angel always says when he comes bringing a message?

"Be not afraid!"

Angels have to say that, of course, because they are frighteningly glorious. Don't believe those pictures of chubby little cherubs with tiny wings. If you saw an angel today, your first reaction wouldn't be, "Awww, how cute!"

But the other reason angels have to say, "Be not afraid!" is because they always come bearing some sort of instruction from God. And God wants us to do things that might seem absolutely terrifying.

Gabriel says it to Mary at the Annunciation. "Be not afraid."

Now think of the rest of the message.

"Don't be afraid, Mary. I'm just here to turn your life upside down and start you on a roller-coaster ride like nothing any mortal woman has ever experienced. Oh, and by the way, there's something you might have a *little* trouble explaining to your fiancé." It sounds as though Mary has plenty to be afraid of.

But Gabriel is right. She really has no reason to be afraid, because God knows how it will all turn out. And it will turn out amazing.

Yes, Mary will witness the death of her son. But then she will see him gloriously resurrected. Yes, she will have to do some hard work. But she will be the Queen of Heaven!

And Mary does respond fearlessly. That doesn't mean she feels no fear, of course. I imagine her feeling quite a bit of anxiety. How will she break the news to Joseph? How is she supposed to bring up the Son of God? What will the gossiping ladies of Nazareth say when they see that she's pregnant?

But I say she responds fearlessly because in spite of whatever fear she might feel, she instantly does what God has asked her to do. "Behold, I am the handmaid of the Lord; let it be to me according to your word." (Luke 1:38)

And once she says that, she's all in.

• • • •

We've just spent some time talking about what's wrong with the world, and about how the Church has the answers to those problems because she has Jesus.

But simply knowing that isn't enough. You have to do something with those answers. You have to make the changes you know need to be made.

That's your mission from God.

And it can be terrifying.

I'm convinced that fear is the number-one thing that holds us back from doing what God wants us to do in the world. It's not always fear of death or dismemberment. Sometimes it's fear of much worse things than that—like making a fool of yourself.

Take an honest look at your own life. How much of what you do is determined by what other people might think of you?

I'm a specialist at making a fool of myself. I go to parishes all over the country to make a fool of myself. There I am, standing in front of hundreds of people, any one of whom might be thinking, "Boy, what an idiot."

I used to care, *a lot*. I used to think about that guy all the time—the guy who was dragged to the parish mission by his family, and he's sitting out there watching me, thinking to himself, "You know, I'd rather die than make an idiot of myself up there like that Leonetti character."

But anymore, I don't care. Not because I'm not passionate (most of the time they have to turn my microphone down), but because I'd rather be a fool for Christ than a fool for something else.

I'm not saying I'm not afraid of anything. I'm afraid of lots of things. And it's OK to be afraid—that's our fallen human nature. We care more about looking cool than we do about how God wants us to live.

But if we go ahead and do what God wants anyway, he will take care of us. He'll give us the strength we need to keep doing what we know we have to do. He may even give us the strength not to feel like complete fools while we're doing it.

And that's what the angel means when he says, "Be not afraid." He doesn't mean, "Control your adrenal glands and achieve a state of complete bodily and mental tranquility." You can't do that. Instead, the angel's message is, "Overcome your fear and do what God wants in spite of it, and have faith that God will take care of you."

• • • •

Fear can be paralyzing. According to the National Institute of Mental Health, nearly one in five Americans will suffer from anxiety serious enough to be described as a "disorder"—something wrong with the way we interact with the world. And it seems as though the more we do to feel safe, the more anxious we get.

And here I am telling you to go out and do the very things that scare you most. What's wrong with me, anyway?

Now, I'm not going to try to tell you that you won't have fears to overcome. But I want you to understand what we're asking of ourselves.

We don't need to be superheroes. We don't need powers beyond mortal strength or wisdom beyond mortal understanding. We don't need to do what can't be done—we just need to make some changes.

So what is the Church asking us to do, then? If the Christian life is really so radically different, isn't it . . . well . . . scary?

Maybe.

But the Church is asking us to trust God and go anyway. It isn't asking us to be some kind of superhuman; it's asking us to be human—to affect the change for Christ in our families, parishes, cities, and world, and to do it with precisely what God has given us.

What Christ wants is for you to live virtue—to live holiness—in a way that maybe you've never lived before. He wants you to live it better today than you did yesterday, and to live it better tomorrow than you did today. Each day builds on the day before. Each layer builds on the layer below.

That's just like what happens in our lives when we choose to go the other way. It doesn't just build up; it can also build down. Why do some young people decide to chase lust rather than Christ, or to choose the bottle rather than Catholicism?

And why do they say, "Well, I go to these retreats and I just don't *feel* anything"? It doesn't take a rocket scientist to figure out that these people have numbed themselves. They've built up so many layers that they've surrounded themselves with a brick wall. And it's shutting our Lord out.

We need to tear down that wall. And we need to *keep* tearing it down; it's not just a one-and-done deal. We know this in our Catholic faith. It's not one of those things in which we just say, "I'm saved," and then everything's OK.

Rather, in most of our lives, in our struggles and our difficulties, we have to start tearing down the walls. We have to start ripping through some of those struggles that we're going through.

And we *will* do that, because when we look at the way we've been living, we know that there's got to be something better than this.

I've never forgotten something John Paul II said at one World Youth Day. He looked out at all those young people, a sea of millions, and he said, "You were made for greater things." He was absolutely right. You were made to be holy, not just to stumble through life oblivious. You are mission. Christ is telling you right now, "I need you."

Can you think of anything more exciting than that? The most radical revolutionary who ever walked on earth is calling you—not just people in general, but you personally—and saying, "I need you. The mission can't happen without you. You have talents and abilities that no one else on earth has. I need you to help me save the world." I don't know about you, but I think I'm sold. Jesus needs me to save the world! Maybe it won't be easy, but it sure will be anything but boring.

That's something to get passionate about.

• • • •

Passion is what we need if we're going to change the world. People are inspired by passion. That's true whether you're talking about religion or anything else.

There were plenty of people who thought racial equality in America would be a good idea. Why did everyone pay attention to Martin Luther King? Because he had passion. He lived his ideals—he didn't just talk about what a good thing it would be if someone did something about injustice. He went to jail. He brushed off death threats. He went where everyone told him not to go, and he brought his message where it most needed to be heard.

How about Mother Teresa? She heard two words on a train one day and believed they were from God: "I thirst." From there she laid the foundation for some of the boldest revolutionaries the twentieth century has known. They're called the Missionaries of Charity.Martin Luther King and Mother Teresa were passionate about what they believed in—so passionate that they weren't afraid, even of death. Even more heroic, they weren't afraid to live for it. Passion gets things done, because it gets people behind you.

It works for the Devil's side, too. But I have a feeling that's not the kind of passion you're hoping for. What you and I want is the kind of passion that gets every good thing done, the kind that made Mother Teresa, a frail little old lady, a flame that shot across the world spreading light wherever she went.

So where do you look for that passion?

You ask for it.

Remember, it was the Holy Spirit that made the apostles into the men they became. Before Pentecost, they just sat around behind locked doors, worrying about getting caught and taken away like Jesus had been. They were afraid to go out into the world and get anything done.

But they prayed. "All these with one accord devoted themselves to prayer, together with the women and Mary the mother of Jesus, and with his brothers." (Acts 1:14)

And the Spirit came at Pentecost.

And after that, there was nothing they couldn't do. By the time the last of the apostles died, there wasn't a corner of the known world that hadn't started to hear the Gospel.

• • • •

And those were just twelve men! I often ponder how so few saints can make such a profound difference in the world. But I think it all goes back to that passion.

If we're going to convince the world of our Lord's love, the truth is, we have to fall in love first.

This means we have to get to know him and let him light our hearts on fire. Truly, it's the only way.

I was giving a talk on atheism at a high school and a kid came up to me and asked me how I knew there was a God.

I had just spent an hour giving these kids all the arguments against atheism, and here he came with this question. It was like he hadn't paid attention at all. What I wanted to say was, "Did you listen to *anything* I just said?"

But then I realized that he was asking something different—not how I knew the *arguments* against atheism that I'd presented, but how I knew *personally* that there really is a God.

I answered him the only way I could: "Because I know him."

If you've ever been to one of my talks, you know that by just about a minute and a half in I'm passionate. But it's not just because it makes sense to me, or because it excites me. It's because I'm in love with Jesus and his Church. And when that happens within us, we can set the world ablaze.

So how do we do it? Where do we start?

We start where the apostles started—with prayer. Faith without prayer is nothing but a hobby.

If I opened up your calendar, I bet I'd see a lot of appointments in it. And I would know each one is important to you, because you've scheduled time for it. But where in your calendars is your prayer scheduled?

Prayer is spelled T-I-M-E. If you put prayer last on your list of priorities, it won't happen. You have to put it first.

Yes, the bills have to be paid. Yes, you have to go to the doctor. You have to get to work on time. You have to get to your Spanish lesson, your soccer game, your neighborhood-watch meeting.

Just make up your mind that prayer is what you do *before* you do these things. You make time to get dressed before then, right? You'd look pretty ridiculous if you didn't. Well, prayer is just as necessary as getting dressed. In fact, it's far more necessary. Make up your mind that prayer is your top priority.

But there's another question that is lurking behind: What do we say when we pray?

I travel a lot. And when I'm home with my family, I often just sit with them, watch my son walk around and knock things over, and put my arm around Teresa. I don't have to say anything (and Teresa prefers it that way).

Start with silence. Pope Benedict XVI once said, "Silence is the language of God."

Our lives are busy and fast. What would seven minutes of silence do for you in your day, in your week, in your life? It would give God room.

We must make room for God in our lives. And that happens first with silence.

Pray with the Scriptures. I like to use my imagination when I pray. There is nothing more exciting to me than putting myself in one of the Gospel stories. I love to close my eyes and imagine myself as the blind man begging Jesus to heal me. I love to read and discover more of the cultural context of what Jesus said.

When I'm at parish missions, I see firsthand the audience's eyes when I break some of these Gospel stories down. They are more interested than I've ever seen, because they suddenly can imagine themselves there, at the most exciting time in the history of the world, the time when the world met God in the flesh. The events aren't just words on a page anymore; they're real things that happened to real people, people just like us.

So I think your imagination can be a big part of your prayer life. If you have trouble talking to Jesus as an abstract idea, try closing your eyes and imagining a scene from the Gospels. Think of Jesus walking with you down the dusty road to Emmaus, explaining the Scriptures to you. Tell him what's on your mind. Maybe he'll tell you what's on his mind, too.

But I know that kind of imaginative prayer doesn't work for everybody. The Catholic Church has all kinds of prayer traditions, because it has all kinds of people. *Catholic* means "universal," after all. There's something for everybody. Learn about those different traditions and try them out. Find what works for you.

The important thing is to pray. Are you afraid to set foot out the door? So were the apostles after Jesus ascended. But they prayed, and the Spirit came to them. The Spirit will come to you, too. But you've got to ask.

•   •   •   •

So what can we actually accomplish when we follow the angel's advice? What can we do when we face the world without giving in to fear?

I'm going to tell you a story. It's one you already know, but maybe you haven't thought about its implications.

Once upon a time, the world was divided between east and west, dictatorships and democracies. All of Eastern Europe and a big chunk of Asia were covered by the mighty Soviet Union and its satellites, the biggest and most powerful empire the world has ever seen. Theoretically, the countries of Eastern Europe—East Germany, Poland, Hungary, Czechoslovakia, and the rest—were independent nations. But really they were part of the vast Soviet Empire. If they actually tried to do anything independent, the Soviet tanks rolled in and made sure they knew who was really in control.

Anyone who lived in the 1970s thought this was the way the world was built. The Soviet Empire was far too huge and powerful for any outside force to challenge successfully, and it would take a miracle to change it from the inside.

But then something absolutely unexpected happened.

Pope John Paul I died in Rome. That was unexpected enough, since he had only been pope for a month. But what happened next completely mesmerized the world. The cardinals met for the second time in weeks and announced their choice: Karol Wojtyla, a Polish cardinal, who took the name

John Paul II. There hadn't been a non-Italian pope since 1523, and this one was from the Communist empire!

Not long after he was elected, the new pope visited his home country, where immense crowds filled the streets of Warsaw to see him. And what did he tell them?

He didn't tell them, "Throw out your atheist dictators." He didn't say, "Take to the streets and take back your country." What he told them was far more revolutionary, because it was the one thing that could actually mobilize a whole population:

"Do not be afraid."

After that, it was only a matter of time. Only ten years after John Paul II told the people, "Do not be afraid," the Communist dictatorships of Europe toppled one after another. And the Soviet tanks didn't roll in to pick them back up.

Sometimes I hear people talking about how America "won" the Cold War. I think those people completely miss the point. The people of Poland won. The people of all those other formerly Communist countries won. They're the ones who stood up and defied the Soviet Empire. No American tanks backed them up. No American air raids held back the Soviet forces. The people of Eastern Europe faced down their dictators, and they won because they suddenly realized that *it was possible to win*. One man came to them and told them, "Do not be afraid." And they listened to his message and took it to heart. They discovered that no matter how many tanks the other side could deploy, it was possible to live life fearlessly.

Is it any wonder the world is calling that man Saint John Paul the Great?

The story of John Paul II and the fall of Communism should be our inspiration. Because people began to live without fear, they were able to destroy the great "evil empire" that had seemed absolutely indestructible.

But what about you? What about the "empire" you're up against?

Do you think your sanctity could destroy it?

We've talked a lot about the saints in this book—how amazing their stories are, what courage they had, and why people admire them so much. And you might be saying to yourself, "I'm a good person most of the time, but I'm not a saint. I'm not *that* holy."

The problem with that line of thinking is we've forgotten our story, the story I spent the first half of this book unpacking. We've forgotten that God has sent an ark to save us like he sent to Noah. Not literally, of course. I'm not saying a boat is going to appear in your driveway soon. The ark God gives you and me is the ark of holiness, the ark of sanctity. Are you willing to get in?

There's no saint who has ever lived who has your DNA—not a single one.

But there could be. God made you to be that saint. When he was making you, he said to himself, "This is a masterpiece. There's no other saint who can be like this one. I know *exactly* what I want this one for."

God didn't make you to throw you away. He made you because he knew that the universe could be much better with you than without you.

Could be—that's the key. God also gave you free will. He won't force you to love him, because that wouldn't really be love, would it? It would be more like force. God wants you to love him, and he wants you to live the life he showed you through his son. But he won't make you do it. You have to answer when he calls you.

That's mission. Christ invites us to a new way of living. And that new way of living is radically different from my way, and our way, and the world's way. It's radically different because it's radically better, and God knows that if you answer the call, you'll be a much happier person.

Notice that I didn't say you'll be more successful, or better-looking. Those things don't make you happy—and again, if you want evidence, I refer you to the celebrity-gossip tabloids at the supermarket checkout counter.

So be not afraid!

And trust that God will take care of you.

I'm not saying it'll be easy. I'm not saying you won't struggle. I'm not saying it won't sometimes be painful.

But I will say this, and I guarantee it: It won't be boring.

CONCLUSION

I've spent most of this book illustrating the big picture, which the world is desperately in need of hearing: God is not boring. And the life he has for you isn't boring either.

That's really what I want to leave you with.

However, I wouldn't be doing the message justice if I didn't lead you to the outlet. After all, the plug is useless without it; there's no power.

• • • •

Despite the way my office usually looks, I'm something of a perfectionist. Rather than seeing the glass as half-full or half-empty, I think about what might make the glass and whatever else is in it a little bit better. I know it drives Teresa nuts, but when I sit in the pew on Sunday morning I'm not judging how bad things are. Actually my parish is really good; otherwise I wouldn't be there. But I'm imagining how much more it could be—if we decided to make it that way, if we decided to do this together.

I go all around the country giving keynotes and parish missions. Generally I spend one to four days speaking about the importance of knowing and living our Catholic faith, the effect it can have on me and those I love, and how it can change the world. Especially after my missions, I like to close with a commission. And as we conclude this book I want to challenge you with it, too. It's the same commission I'm challenged with by those who love me. But you have to know one thing before I begin: It's not a commission to make us comfortable. After all, love hurts.

Are you ready?

Dream with me.

What would the Catholic Church look like if being a Catholic actually meant something—*really* meant something, so that our friends and neighbors who know nothing of the faith could see the difference? What if everyone could tell that what it means to be a member of the Catholic Church is to take one's faith life very seriously, to know God in a radical way and live that way every day? What would the Church look like if every Catholic took on a patron saint as their own special model and guide, if we prayed for their intercession before every major activity, and if we strove to imitate their strongest virtues and taught our children to do the same? What would our Church look like if everyone was so proud to be a part of it that they would beg as many of their friends and family as they possibly could to give it a try, even for just one week?

Imagine ushers at parishes around the world not simply smiling while handing us the bulletin after Mass to place in the backseat of our car, but calling us by name and asking how our week was.

Imagine every Catholic singing in the pews during Mass, whatever the style and however good or bad the organist or other musicians are. Imagine a homily so good that we find ourselves still talking about it Wednesday evening. Imagine people from other faith denominations all over your city coming to listen to "that one priest" preach.

Imagine a Church where our parish's intentions are prayed *intentionally,* by everyone, and our concern for our neighbors is so real that we find ourselves praying for them and their intentions at our family dinners.

Imagine a Church where at Communion time millions around the world approach slowly and reverently, and receive the Eucharist as though it's the most important thing they will do all week.

Imagine if in your parish every time we heard a baby cry our first instinct and that of the people around us was to give thanks to God for the gift of the baby, and not to wonder why the parents haven't taken her out of the church yet.

Imagine every parish around the world full fifteen minutes before Mass, with parishioners prayerfully preparing for the true presence of Jesus to enter into their souls, and where people stay five minutes after to give thanks to God for the gift they have received.

What would our Church look like if daily Mass in your parish looked like a Sunday? What if daily Mass were more than a few people and the schoolchildren showing up once a week? Can you imagine showing up on Saturday to help with a car wash or parish cleanup and seeing as many people in line for confession as at the penance services during Advent or Lent?

What would the Church look like if every parish around the world were known as the premier place in their city for social outreach, feeding the poor, helping those who are pregnant and in crisis, assisting immigrants, and helping people save their houses?

What would the Church look like if everyone belonged to a Bible study as well as taking part in some special ministry of prayer?

What if every Catholic in your parish volunteered to take Communion to some elderly or homebound person, reminding them that they are loved and not forgotten by the Church?

What if you felt so confident in the prayer lives of your fellow parishioners that you genuinely felt comfortable asking them to pray for your specific struggles or concerns, and in addition, took their prayer requests as seriously as anything else you are asked to do all week?

What if instead of passing by our priest after Mass with a handshake and smile, we asked him what specific parish needs we can fulfill that week? What if every Catholic around the world started to treat their priest as though he really were the spiritual father of their parish and of their family; if we invited him out to eat, had him bless us and our kids before he left the house, and went to him first when we had some serious personal problem?

What would the Catholic Church look like if the priests, deacons, religious, and lay ministers were all so impressive that every Catholic parent encouraged their kids to consider a religious vocation instead of trying to steer them away from it because of money?

What would the Catholic Church look like if every parish around the world were really beginning to make us into saints? What would you begin to look like? How would it change your marriage? How would it change your kids?

So when I sit in the pew before Mass with a look on my face that might be hard to read, I'm imagining things being different, being even better than they are now.

But it's not because I'm disappointed in Catholics around the world. It's because every time I gather with God's people for Holy Mass, I see the true potential within me and within you. Why? Because God's there, and this is what God longs to do with us.

Saint Irenaeus says, "The glory of God is man fully alive."

Just imagine: What would the Catholic Church look like if every man, woman, and child, every family, every couple, every single, every priest, every religious, every layperson, everyone on the books at your parish were made just a little more alive each day, each week, each year?

I'll tell you what it would look like: It would change the world.

It's time we got to work.

Endnotes

1. Julian the Apostate, *On the Duties of a Priest* (extracted from the *Epistle of Themistius)*. Adapted from *Select Works of the Emperor Julian,* translated by John Duncombe from the French of the Abbe de la Bleterie. London: J. Nichols, 1784.

2. *St. Augustine's Confessions.* Book I, Chapter 6. Adapted from the translation (by Bishop Richard Challoner) published anonymously in Dublin: Farrell Kiernan, 1770.

3. *St. Augustine's Confessions.* Book VIII, Chapter 12. Adapted from the translation (by Bishop Richard Challoner) published anonymously in Dublin: Farrell Kiernan, 1770.

4. *St. Augustine's Confessions.* Book VIII, Chapter 12. Adapted from the translation (by Bishop Richard Challoner) published anonymously in Dublin: Farrell Kiernan, 1770.

5. Adapted from the translation by the Rev. R. E. Wallis in *The Passion of the Holy Martyrs Perpetua and Felicitas.* An appendix to *The Ante-Nicene Fathers,* Vol. III, edited by the Rev. Alexander Roberts and James Donaldson. New York: Charles Scribner's Sons, 1903.

ABOUT THE AUTHOR

JON LEONETTI is an international Catholic speaker, author and radio host who conveys a message of lasting fulfillment in Jesus Christ. Jon desires to cultivate an intimate relationship with Jesus and help others do the same through prayer, the Sacraments, family life, Mary and the saints. Engaging Catholics in all walks of life, Jon's keynote presentations and parish missions help thousands of Catholics each year discover the freedom Christ offers by way of his life and love.

Jon is a regular guest and contributor to the nations top Catholic websites, blogs, and radio shows helping others to better fall in love and stay in love with the living God.

In addition to his Catholic faith, Jon enjoys reading, sports, exercising, coffee, and most of all, spending time with his wife Teresa and their son Joseph. Jon is currently pursuing a masters degree in Moral Theology.

Learn more by visiting Jon's website: www.JonLeonetti.com

Blessed.

THE DYNAMIC CATHOLIC FIRST COMMUNION & FIRST RECONCILIATION EXPERIENCE

There's never been anything like this for children: World-class animation. Workbooks with 250 hand-painted works of art. Catechist-friendly leader guides, and incredible content. Blessed isn't just different, it's groundbreaking.

**Request your FREE First Communion Program Pack &
First Reconciliation Program Pack
at *DynamicCatholic.com/BlessedPack***

EACH PROGRAM PACK INCLUDES:

- 1 DVD SET (42 ANIMATED SHORT FILMS)
- 1 STUDENT WORKBOOK
- 1 LEADER GUIDE
- 1 CHILDREN'S PRAYER PROCESS CARD

Just pay shipping.

Dynamic Catholic
Be Bold. Be Catholic.®

N O T E S

Mission of the Family
Jon Leonetti

Get a FREE* copy at **DynamicCatholic.com**.
Shipping and handling not included.

HAVE YOU EVER WONDERED HOW THE CATHOLIC FAITH COULD HELP YOU LIVE BETTER?

How it could help you find more *joy* at work, *manage* your personal finances, *improve* your marriage, or make you a *better* parent?

THERE IS GENIUS IN CATHOLICISM.

When *Catholicism* is lived as it is intended to be, it elevates every part of our lives. It may sound simple, but they say *genius is taking something complex and making it simple.*

Dynamic Catholic started with a dream: to help ordinary people discover the *genius of Catholicism.*

Wherever you are in your journey, we want to meet you there and walk with you, *step by step*, helping you to discover God and become *the-best-version-of-yourself.*

To find more helpful resources, visit us online at DynamicCatholic.com.

Dynamic Catholic

FEED YOUR SOUL.